THE STATE OF THE WORLD'S CHILDREN
SPECIAL EDITION

Foreword

A historic decision was made on 20 November 1989, when world leaders adopted the Convention on the Rights of the Child in the UN General Assembly. Since its inception 20 years ago, the Convention has become the most-ratified human rights treaty in history. This is testament to the common understanding among countries and communities that children have the right to survive and develop; to be protected from violence, abuse and exploitation; and for their views to be respected and actions concerning them to be taken in their best interests. Meeting children's rights is not only fundamental for their development and well-being, it is also pivotal to creating the world envisioned by the Millennium Declaration – a world of peace, equity, security, respect for the environment and shared responsibility – in short, a world fit for children.

Much has been achieved during the past 20 years. The annual number of under-five deaths has fallen from around 12.5 million in 1990 to less than 9 million in 2008. Between 1990 and 2006, 1.6 billion people worldwide gained access to improved water sources. Globally, around 84 per cent of primary-school-age children are attending school, and gender gaps in primary-school enrolment are shrinking across the developing world. The fight against the AIDS pandemic is intensifying and yielding results, with steady increases in the number of pregnant women with HIV receiving antiretroviral drugs to prevent mother-to-child transmission of the virus, and growing numbers of newborns and infants being tested and then also receiving the full course of medication to protect them from HIV.

Advances in child protection and participation, although often less measurable due to gaps in data, have been no less significant. In the past two decades, around 70 countries have incorporated children's codes into national legislation based on the Convention's provisions. Expanded international household surveys have, since the mid-1990s, begun to provide regular estimates of several important protection issues, such as child marriage, female genital mutilation/cutting, and, more recently, attitudes towards domestic violence and child discipline. Paradigms such as the protective environment are providing a firm basis for national child-protection systems. Awareness of and advocacy on child protection issues have increased markedly. On two key issues – children in armed conflict and violence against children – the naming of UN special representatives have underscored that increased attention and determined effort.

The agenda for children's rights is far from complete. Millions of children remain without the essential services to help ensure their survival, reduce their vulnerability to disease and undernutrition, provide access to improved water and sanitation, and enable them to obtain quality education. Many children lack the protective environment required to safeguard them from violence, abuse, exploitation, discrimination and neglect. The problem of violence against children is particularly alarming, with between 500 million and 1.5 billion children estimated to experience violence annually. Its consequences are pernicious, with many child victims experiencing long-standing physical and mental health difficulties later in life.

The continents of Africa and Asia, and especially the regions of sub-Saharan Africa and South Asia, have the greatest concentrations of absolute deprivations of child rights and will demand particular attention in the coming years. All countries and regions face the task of tackling the increasingly apparent disparities among economic and social groups in access to and outcomes for children's health, education and protection.

As it enters its 21st year as a UN treaty, the Convention on the Rights of the Child faces the challenge of consolidating the undoubted gains in child rights of the past, while addressing the risks and grasping the opportunities of the present and future. The recent global economic downturn exposes many to greater hunger, undernutrition, lack of opportunity and hardship. Children and young people are most at risk from this poverty penalty, with almost 45 per cent of the world's population currently under the age of 25.

There is mounting disquiet about climate change and its impact on health, water security and food production; at least 18 violent conflicts since 1990 have involved a struggle for resources. Increased competition for resources will take place in a world with a burgeoning population, potentially exacerbating equities in income and access to vital services. Meeting these challenges will require us to unite for children through judicious investment and broad collaboration, with children and women as key partners.

Evidence has shown that investing in child rights is both a responsibility and an opportunity. It is a responsibility because poverty, undernutrition and other deprivations undermine children's abilities to develop to their full potentials. It is an opportunity because the gains achieved through better nutrition, primary health care, education and protection for children are likely to be far greater and long-lasting than in almost any other area of development.

Broad collaboration is vital to the implementation of the Convention's principles and the rights it prescribes. Collaboration in health, education, protection and participation at international and national levels have expanded in recent years, offering the promise of accelerated progress on child rights and towards internationally agreed development goals.

Children's participation empowers them in their own development and protection. Initiatives such as the 2002 UN Special Session on Children, the annual Junior 8 meetings that run concurrently with the G-8 summits, and numerous child friendly cities programmes are showing the benefits of respecting and encouraging the views and participation of children in decision-making forums.

Empowering women and eliminating gender discrimination produces a double dividend – fulfilling the rights of women and also helping to save and improve the lives of children. Evidence shows that when women are educated and empowered to participate in decision-making in the household, workplace and political sphere – secure from violence, exploitation and discrimination – children and families benefit. Both boys and girls are more likely to have access to adequate nutrition, quality health care and education; girls are also more likely to delay marriage and enjoy greater opportunities for development and growth. Educating girls and ensuring their protection and participation is therefore of pivotal importance to the child rights agenda.

The challenge for the next 20 years is to build on the progress achieved, working together to reach those children who are still being denied their rights to survival, development, protection and participation. The Convention on the Rights of the Child stands as a universal standard for building a better world – a world in which the best interests of children are a primary concern of all.

Ann M. Veneman
Executive Director, UNICEF

CONTENTS

THE STATE OF THE WORLD'S CHILDREN

SPECIAL EDITION

Celebrating 20 Years of the Convention on the Rights of the Child

The Timeless Relevance of The Convention

On 20 November 2009, the global community celebrates the 20th anniversary of the adoption by the United Nations General Assembly of the Convention on the Rights of the Child. This unique document outlines universal standards for the care, treatment and protection of all individuals below age 18. It is the most widely endorsed human rights treaty in history, currently ratified by 193 States parties.

During the past two decades, the Convention has transformed the way children are viewed and treated throughout the world. It has exerted a pervasive and profound influence on national and international legislation, policy and programmes, public and private institutions, families, communities and individuals. And it has supported marked advances in survival, development, protection and participation across the world.

Despite the numerous challenges that remain in realizing children's rights, the Convention offers a vision of a world in which all children survive and develop, and are protected, respected and encouraged to participate in the decisions that affect them. This vision promotes a world of peace, tolerance, equity, respect for human rights and shared responsibility – in short, a world fit for children.

The evolution of international standards on child rights

1924

The League of Nations adopts the Geneva Declaration on the Rights of the Child. The declaration establishes children's rights to means for material, moral and spiritual development; special help when hungry, sick, disabled or orphaned; first call on relief when in distress; freedom from economic exploitation; and an upbringing that instils a sense of social responsibility.

1948

The UN General Assembly passes the Universal Declaration of Human Rights, which refers in article 25 to childhood as "entitled to special care and assistance."

1959

The UN General Assembly adopts the Declaration of the Rights of the Child, which recognizes rights such as freedom from discrimination and the rights to a name and nationality. It also specifically enshrines children's rights to education, health care and special protection.

The Convention on the Rights of the Child (henceforth referred to as 'the Convention') was adopted by the UN General Assembly on 20 November 1989 and entered into force on 2 September 1990. It is the most comprehensive human rights treaty and legal instrument for the promotion and protection of children's rights. Although there are provisions protecting child rights in other international human rights instruments, the Convention is the first to articulate the entire complement of rights relevant to children – economic, social, cultural, civil and political. It was also the first international instrument to explicitly recognize children as social actors and active holders of their own rights.

Under the provisions of the treaty, States parties are legally obliged to fulfil the rights of every child. The Convention comprises 54 articles and is based on four core principles: non-discrimination; best interests of the child; the right to life, survival and development; and respect for the views of children. Its broad scope and the importance it places on the agency of the child make it timelessly relevant to all actions that intend to promote, protect and fulfil children's rights.

The Convention is a powerful addition to the international human rights framework. Although it has been in existence for only two decades, it has achieved near-universal acceptance, having been ratified by 193 countries by 2009, with only two outstanding: Somalia and the United States, both of which have indicated their support by signing the treaty. The influence of the Convention and its Optional Protocols is already pervasive across continents and regions, countries and communities, and it will clearly remain the children's Magna Carta for decades – possibly even centuries – to come.

The Convention has significantly reaffirmed and enriched human rights. It reaffirms by applying many of the core principles of earlier international human rights instruments, such as universality and non-discrimination, directly to children. It enriches by consolidating and amplifying the provisions that are included in other human rights instruments, specifying the responsibilities and duties of States parties towards children. It incorporates rights for children that were not widely articulated – notably the right to participation – and stipulates that the best interests of the child should be a primary consideration in all actions towards them. It stresses that accountability for child rights lies with the duty bearers, including States parties, families and guardians, who are entrusted with ensuring that children's rights are realized.

The full significance of the Convention extends well beyond its legislative implications. It has also helped transform attitudes towards childhood. In effect, the Convention has set the *terms of childhood*, outlining the minimum standards for the treatment, care, survival, development, protection and participation that are due every individual under age 18. Its articles reinforce a common understanding among societies that to fulfil the rights of children it is imperative to protect childhood as a period that is separate from adulthood, to define a time in which children can grow, learn, play and develop.

1966

The International Covenant on Civil and Political Rights and the International Covenant on Economic, Social and Cultural Rights are adopted. The covenants advocate protection for children from exploitation and promote the right to education.

1973

The International Labour Organizations adopts Convention No. 138 on the Minimum Age for Admission to Employment, which sets 18 years as the minimum age for work that might be hazardous to an individual's health, safety or morals.

1979

The UN General Assembly adopts the Convention on the Elimination of All Forms of Discrimination Against Women, which provides protection for the human rights of girls as well as women. It also declares 1979 as International Year of the Child, which sets in motion the working group to draft a legally binding Convention on the Rights of the Child.

Under the Convention, children are rights holders rather than objects of charity. Fulfilling these rights is no longer an option for States parties but an obligation that governments have pledged to meet. Equally important is the optimism, clarity and steadfastness that the Convention captures for the future – that one day all children will enjoy a childhood with full respect for their rights, their basic needs provided for, protected from violence, abuse, exploitation, neglect and discrimination, and empowered to participate meaningfully in all decisions that affect their lives.

In its preamble and throughout its articles the Convention underscores the fundamental role of the family in the growth and well-being of children, recognizing the crucial importance of a loving, harmonious and understanding family environment for the full development of children. It obliges States parties to provide the family with all the means necessary to realize its responsibilities.

To celebrate 20 years of the Convention, the United Nations Children's Fund (UNICEF) is dedicating a special edition of its flagship report *The State of the World's Children* to child rights. Specifically, this report addresses questions that arise as the treaty reaches its own 'coming of age'. First, what difference has the Convention made to the lives of children during the past two decades? Second, what is its role and relevance in the face of recent and severe global food, fuel and financial crises? Finally, what role can it have over the next 20 years and beyond in an increasingly populous, urbanized and environmentally challenged world?

These questions are examined in this opening chapter by a review of the evolution of international standards on child rights, acknowledging the Convention's roots in the campaigns that began in the early 1900s as well as the unstinting work during the 1980s of individuals and civil society organizations that enabled a charter for child rights to become reality. The report then proceeds to review the core principles of the Convention, assessing their impact on children's well-being and human development. In succeeding chapters, the challenges to furthering child rights during the next two decades are surveyed – first through a selection of guest essays, and then in a final section that outlines the threats and opportunities ahead and charts a path to a better future for the world's children. Selected county panels are employed throughout the report to highlight the progress on, challenges of, risks to and opportunities for child rights across the world's continents and regions.

The commemorations in 2009 of the Convention and other landmarks for child rights are celebrations of humanity and honour the collective will, understanding and creativity that make social and economic progress possible. Many elements – religion and learning, innovation and globalization, civil rights movements and non-governmental organizations, and the determination of families, communities and individuals, children and adolescents – have helped ensure, and will continue to make certain, that the Convention's articles translate into action and results.

The evolution of international standards on child rights

1989
The UN General Assembly unanimously approves the Convention on the Rights of the Child, which enters into force the following year.

1990
The 1990 World Summit for Children adopts the World Declaration on the Survival, Protection and Development of Children along with a plan of action for implementing it in the 1990s.

1999
The International Labour Organization adopts Convention No. 182 concerning the Prohibition and Immediate Action for the Elimination of the Worst Forms of Child Labour.

The early movement for child rights

The Convention's adoption in 1989 marked the culmination of a long process of articulating and consolidating child rights in the international arena that stretched back to the early years of the 20th century.

The emergence of international momentum

The end of the First World War marked the point when newly formed international organizations began to articulate codes of human rights. The new bodies gave some consideration to the specific rights of children; for example, the newly formed International Labour Office (now Organization) concentrated its earliest conventions on asserting the rights of child workers, as in the Night Work of Young Persons (Industry) Convention of 1919 and the Minimum Age (Agriculture) Convention of 1921.[1] Much of the international legislation introduced between the world wars, however, did not explicitly specify rights for children as distinct from those of adults.

The first formal conceptualization of child rights by the nascent international organizations derived from the work of Eglantyne Jebb, who founded the Save the Children Fund in England in 1919 and established the Save the Children International Union in Geneva the following year. Save the Children was founded to raise money for emergency aid to children suffering the consequences of World War I.[2] In 1923, Jebb declared her position on child rights in the following statement: "The moment appears to me to have come when we can no longer expect to conduct large relief actions. If we wish nevertheless to go on working for the children ... the only way to do it seems to be to evoke a cooperative effort of the nations to safeguard their own children on constructive rather than on charitable lines. I believe we should claim certain rights for the children and labour for their universal recognition."[3]

To that end, the Save the Children International Union drafted a succinct declaration asserting child rights and persuaded the League of Nations to adopt it as the Geneva Declaration of the Rights of the Child on 26 September 1924. The Geneva Declaration articulated five core principles, underscoring the child's right to the means for material and spiritual development; help when hungry, sick, disabled, orphaned or delinquent; priority relief in times of distress; protection from exploitation; and a socially oriented upbringing.[4]

Child rights in the era of the United Nations

Just as the aftermath of the First World War prompted new efforts at international cooperation and regulation aimed at averting conflict, so the Second World War ushered in the United Nations. In 1946, the International Union for Child Welfare (IUCW) – a merger between the Save the Children International Union and the Brussels-based International Association for Child Welfare – pressed the United Nations to endorse the Geneva Declaration.

For its part, the United Nations was more concerned with articulating the all-embracing principles of the 1948 Universal Declaration of Human Rights, and the idea of a renewed document dedicated to child rights was instead

2000

The UN General Assembly adopts two Optional Protocols to the Convention on the Rights of the Child: one on the involvement of children in armed conflict, the other on the sale of children, child prostitution and child pornography.

2002

The UN General Assembly holds a Special Session on Children, meeting for the first time to specifically discuss children's issues. Hundreds of children participate as members of official delegations, and world leaders commit themselves to a compact on child rights, 'A World Fit for Children.'

2007

The five-year follow-up to the UN General Assembly Special Session on Children ends with a Declaration on Children adopted by more than 140 governments. The Declaration acknowledges progress achieved and the challenges that remain, and reaffirms commitment to the World Fit for Children compact, the Convention and its Optional Protocols.

taken up by the IUCW itself, which updated the earlier declaration and reiterated the notable principle that "mankind owes to the child the best that it has to give."[5]

The United Nations did not adopt its own declaration of child rights until 20 November 1959. The General Assembly's endorsement was significant because it underscored the need for a separate consideration of child rights rather than assuming that these would be taken care of within the broad ambit of international human rights instruments. The Declaration of the Rights of the Child placed stronger emphasis on children's emotional well-being and asserted children's right to be "among the first to receive protection and relief" in emergencies – a phrase that was to be echoed two decades later in UNICEF's slogan 'First Call for Children'. These changes aside, the 1959 document remained fixed in a welfarist approach, aiming to safeguard and protect children, with little emphasis on empowering them as well.

During the 1960s and 1970s, the movement for child rights was rooted in the work of non-governmental organizations (NGOs), which spurred the next great step forward. The NGOs encouraged the United Nations to declare 1979 as the International Year of the Child in an attempt to raise the profile of children's issues. Once this was agreed to, the Government of Poland submitted a draft convention on child rights to the UN Commission on Human Rights. It soon became clear that more time and greater preparation were required for this document to become finalized. As a result, the Commission agreed that an open-ended working group should be entrusted with revising the draft.

The process took a decade, partly because writing a treaty that addresses many areas of social and cultural interpretation is delicate work. Sensitivities also emerged when governments became involved with such issues as child discipline, which many considered to lie within the purview of the family, not the State.

For its part, UNICEF placed less emphasis on the value and practical utility of child rights at that time. During much of the 1980s, the organization was dedicated to its own paradigm, which it championed and shared with a number of partners and allies: the child survival and development revolution. This movement was responsible for a major mobilization of support and action to reduce child mortality and morbidity in the developing world, particularly the application of basic preventive and curative measures such as immunization, oral rehydration therapy, growth monitoring and promotion of breastfeeding.

By 1987, building on the spirit of primary health care that UNICEF had jointly introduced with the World Health Organization (WHO) at the Alma-Ata Conference in 1978, the organization had become more oriented towards the conclusion that the prospects for child survival and development could be enhanced only if they were given due weight within an international instrument embedding child rights in law. UNICEF's support, thereafter, lent considerable impetus to passage of the draft convention through the UN approval process.

The Convention on the Rights of the Child was adopted by the UN General Assembly on 20 November 1989 – exactly 30 years after the 1959 Declaration of the Rights of the Child

© UNICEF/NYHQ2005-2251/Giacomo Pirozzi

The four core principles of the Convention – non-discrimination, best interests of the child, right to life, survival and development, and respect for the views of the child – should guide actions in all matters concerning children. *Children play with colourful blocks at an early childhood development centre in the rural village of Ajmou in Meknes-Tafilalet Region, Morocco.*

had been accepted. Its landmark status was confirmed almost immediately; on the day it was opened for signature in January 1990, 61 countries signed. Furthermore, the Convention was ratified in record time by the required minimum number of States parties (20) and entered into force in September 1990; it was celebrated later that month during another unique event: the World Summit for Children, held at UN Headquarters in New York. The Summit added political weight to the Convention, and in the Plan of Action for Implementing the World Declaration on the Survival, Protection and Development of Children in the 1990s the 71 heads of state and government in attendance called on all governments to promote the "earliest possible" ratification and implementation of the Convention.

Since the early 1990s, the lexicon and provisions of the Convention have been incorporated into national and regional legislation, declarations, charters and manifestos across the world. In 2000, the UN General Assembly adopted two Optional Protocols to the Convention, on the Involvement of Children in Armed Conflict, and on the Sale of Children, Child Prostitution and Child Pornography. In 2002, world leaders made a commitment to fulfil child rights at the 2002 UN Special Session on Children, encapsulating their determination in a compact entitled 'A World Fit for Children'. These statements urged governments to complete the agenda of the 1990 World Summit, adhere to the standards of the Convention and achieve internationally agreed development objectives and goals – including those incorporated in the 2000 UN Millennium Declaration.

A similar call to action was made at the close of the World Fit for Children +5 special session in December 2007, when a new 'declaration on children' was adopted by more than 140 governments. This latest declaration acknowledges the progress achieved towards meeting child rights and the challenges that persist. It reaffirms commitment to the World Fit for Children compact as well as to the Convention of the Rights of the Child and its Optional Protocols.

The core principles of the Convention

Whereas the 1924 Geneva Declaration and 1959 Declaration of the Rights of the Child expressed the aspirations of the international community concerning child rights, the Convention and its Optional Protocols are legal instruments, and ratifying nations are committed to realizing their provisions. States parties are required to report regularly to the Committee on the Rights of the Child, the body entrusted with monitoring the implementation of the Convention and its Optional Protocols by States parties. The Committee's 18 members also provide States parties with guidance on how to interpret and apply the treaty.

But the Convention is more than a treaty with a monitoring arm; it is a far-reaching opus on the care and protection of children in practical and moral terms. The Convention sets out common standards, yet recognizes that to ensure ownership and relevance, each State party must seek its own way of implementing the treaty. Guidance for national implementation rests on General Comments and the general measures of implementation established by the Committee on the Rights of the Child (*see panel, page 8*) as well as on the foundation of the four core principles:

- Non-discrimination, or universality (article 2)
- Best interests of the child (article 3)
- Right to life, survival and development (article 6)
- Respect for the views of the child (article 12).

Non-discrimination: The rights guaranteed by the Convention are afforded to all children without exception. Article 2

Optional Protocols to the Convention

There are two Optional Protocols to the Convention on the Rights of the Child, both adopted by the UN General Assembly on 25 May 2000. These are the Optional Protocol on the Sale of Children, Child Prostitution and Child Pornography, which came into force on 18 January 2002, and the Optional Protocol on the Involvement of Children in Armed Conflict, which entered into force on 12 February 2002. The Optional Protocols were drafted on issues for which States parties felt ready to adopt stronger commitments than those outlined in the Convention.

Optional Protocol on the Involvement of Children in Armed Conflict

The Convention's consensual drafting process resulted in the minimum age for the involvement of children in armed forces being set at 15 years – an age deemed far too young by many countries. The Optional Protocol requires States parties to prohibit the conscription of anyone under 18, adopt all feasible measures to ensure that voluntarily recruited soldiers under the age of 18 do not fight, and criminalize the recruitment of children under 18 by rebel groups.

The protocol resolved the contradiction in the Convention that did not afford soldiers under 18 the same rights and protection as all other children, establishing a legal norm and international standard that makes it easier to hold nations accountable and encouraging the passing of national laws in accordance with its principles. By July 2009, it had been ratified by 128 countries and signed by a further 28.

Optional Protocol on the Sale of Children, Child Prostitution and Child Pornography

The Optional Protocol on the Sale of Children, Child Prostitution and Child Pornography was devised to strengthen protection for children against these forms of exploitation. Among its provisions are recommendations about the criminalization of such practices; procedures for extradition of those guilty of such offences; calls for international co-operation in tracking and prosecuting offenders; procedures for protecting and assisting child victims; and calls for the promotion of public awareness.

The Optional Protocol on the Sale of Children, Child Prostitution and Child Pornography has succeeded in raising international awareness of the complex issues involved and in influencing national governments' attempts to pass and enforce relevant legislation. By July 2009, the Optional Protocol had been ratified by 132 countries and signed by a further 29.

A peculiarity of the Optional Protocols is that they contain a unique provision that allows them to be ratified by the United States and Somalia, the two countries that have not ratified the Convention. The US Government ratified both Optional Protocols on 23 December 2002; Somalia has signed but not ratified the Optional Protocol on the Involvement of Children in Armed Conflict.

See References, pages 90–92.

---

affirms that States parties "shall respect and ensure the rights set forth in the present Convention to each child within their jurisdiction without discrimination of any kind, irrespective of the child's or his or her parent's or legal guardian's race, colour, sex, language, religion, political or other opinion, national, ethnic or social origin, property, disability, birth or other status."

This universal application today is a core element of any human rights instrument, but in 1959, a separate provision in a draft version of the UN Declaration of the Rights of the Child affirming equality of rights for children born inside and outside marriage was removed from the document. That the principle of non-discrimination is of paramount importance becomes clear when considering, for example, the situation of a child living with disability, an undocumented migrant or a child orphaned by AIDS. Children must also be protected from discrimination that is based on the beliefs of their parents, other family members or legal guardians. The principle of non-discrimination echoes the ethos of the 1965 Convention on the Elimination of Racial Discrimination and the 1979 Convention on the Elimination of All Forms of Discrimination against Women (hereafter referred to as CEDAW).

Disparities in the realization of child rights are apparent in all countries. Even as global economic growth during the 1990s and for much of this decade led to remarkable reductions in absolute poverty in many developing countries – most notably China and India – gaps in maternal, newborn and child health care and in education enrolment among income and population groups have widened markedly. There is concern among child rights advocates that the recent global economic crises may result in further widening of these gaps

The Committee on the Rights of the Child

As with other core international human rights instruments, implementation of the Convention and its two Optional Protocols is overseen by a committee: the Committee on the Rights of the Child, established by article 43 of the treaty. The inaugural Committee, elected in early 1991, was composed of experts from 10 countries and a variety of professional backgrounds, including human rights, international law and juvenile justice. It has since expanded to 18 members, following an amendment to article 43 in November 2002.

The Committee convenes its sessions in Geneva three times a year, in January, May and September; each session lasts four weeks. In addition to monitoring the Convention's implementation, the Committee provides guidance on its interpretation through periodic issuance of General Comments on articles and issues, and also convenes days of general discussion.

In ratifying the Convention, countries agree to submit regular progress reports to the Committee, the first within two years of ratification and subsequent ones every five years thereafter. Each report contains detailed background information about the country in question and offers an account of its progress and constraints in implementing the Convention's articles. Additional progress reports are required of countries that are party to the Optional Protocols.

Governments are advised to concentrate their reports on 'factors and difficulties' that they have encountered in implementing the Convention's provisions and in setting specific goals for accelerating progress. The Committee openly welcomes alternative reports from non-governmental organizations within the country; these often – although not necessarily – follow the same format as the main country report and attempt to address similar issues. In addition, key UN organizations – including UNICEF – may also contribute their own perspective on the situation of children in the reporting country.

The Committee appoints two rapporteurs to undertake a comprehensive examination of each report and associated documentation and then drafts a list of key issues and questions for discussion with the representatives of the State party. The emphasis is on 'constructive dialogue'. At the end of the dialogue, the Committee holds a private meeting to finalize its concluding observations. These usually include acknowledgement of positive steps that have been taken, identify problematic areas that require greater effort, and provide advice on practical measures that could be adopted to improve child rights. Concluding observations can also address any point that the Committee considers important for the protection and promotion of child rights. This may entail, for example, requests for policy changes or endorsements of points made by non-governmental organizations.

The concluding observations are made public to enable the press and other groups in civil society to exert pressure for their implementation. In practice, although the Committee can appoint a rapporteur to follow up on relevant issues in the five-year period between reports, non-governmental organizations play a vital part in both monitoring governments' performance and offering appropriate support as they seek to fulfil their obligations to children. In recent years, regional and subregional workshops on implementation of the concluding observations have been organized by the Treaties and Council Branch of the Office of the High Commissioner for Human Rights in Geneva, in cooperation with a host government and UN organs. These workshops, which are held for a group of countries, bring together a diverse range of participants including governmental officials, representatives of national human rights institutions, non-governmental organizations and UN agencies, funds and programmes.

See References, pages 90–92.

unless corrective action is taken to realize the rights of marginalized and impoverished children, who are most at risk of missing out. (*See section on disparities, pages 17–19, and the panel on the potential impact of the global economic crisis on child rights in Chapter 3, page 62.*)

The best interests of the child: Article 3 states, "In all actions concerning children, whether undertaken by public or private social welfare institutions, courts of law, administrative authorities or legislative bodies, the best interests of the child shall be a primary consideration." This second key principle underpins the legal protection and evidence-based care of children.

The 'best interests' principle requires governments or other stakeholders to review any of their actions for the impact on children. This principle has proved to be a vital influence on legislation, strategies, policies and programmes in support of child rights. It has been especially useful in legal judgements and among social welfare institutions that are required to balance competing concerns – for example, in divorce cases or cases concerning the custody of children. In a growing number of countries, monitoring of government with respect to child rights is performed by a specialized institution, such as Norway's Ombudsman and New Zealand's Commissioner for Child Rights. Some countries also have parliamentary oversight committees that examine progress on child rights.

Right to life, survival and development: Article 6 states that "every child has the inherent right to life" and that States parties "shall ensure to the maximum extent possible the survival and development of the child." The right to survival and development is closely linked to the rights of the child to the enjoyment of the highest attainable standard of health, to health services and to an adequate standard of living. Within the UN context, led by the World Health Organization and UNICEF in particular, measures to ensure survival include growth monitoring, oral rehydration and disease control, breastfeeding, immunization, nutrition, birth spacing and women's literacy. The primary health care approach, also championed by WHO and UNICEF, emphasizes the interconnectedness of essential health care, adequate nutrition, improved water and sanitation and hygiene, sound infrastructure and community partnerships in health. Education has become a cornerstone of child development, with lifelong benefits for individuals and families.

Respect for the views of the child: Rather than being affirmed by a specific article of the Convention, children's right to have their views heard and respected in matters concerning them – according to their age and maturity – is guaranteed by a wide range of provisions. One of the most pivotal is article 12, which holds that States parties "shall assure to the child who is capable of forming his or her own views the right to express those views freely in all matters affecting the child, the views of the child being given due weight in accordance with the age and maturity of the child." Article 12 places an obligation on government to ensure that children's views are sought and considered. This principle also applies in any proceeding affecting them.

A range of civil freedoms for children is also articulated in the Convention, including freedom of expression (article 13), thought and religion (14), association and assembly (15) and access to information (17). These 'participation rights' have spurred greater inclusion of children's voices in development efforts that affect them, from local projects such as peer education and the construction of child-friendly schools to international children's congresses, interventions before parliaments or the UN General Assembly, and

dialogue with world leaders at the G8 Summits. Children's participation has also influenced such key processes as the recommendations of the UN Secretary-General's Study on Violence against Children.

The impact of the Convention on national legislation for child rights

The influence of the Convention has been pervasive in the 20 years since its adoption. It is seen in the increased usage of 'child rights' language in the vernacular of national and international legal documents, policies, programmes and advocacy on security, human rights and development, and in the media. Given the Convention's wide-ranging provisions, a multidimensional approach is useful in assessing its impact on the full range of attitudes, practices, legislation, policies and outcomes that affect children's survival, development and well-being. It is possible to examine the evidence available on these areas since 1990, and to form a general assessment on the extent to which the Convention's articles are being implemented, and how consistently and fully.

One way to assess the impact of the Convention is to consider the extent to which its core principles and other articles have been incorporated within countries' constitutions or legal systems. In its review of States parties' reports, the Committee on the Rights of the Child has consistently emphasized the importance of ensuring that national legislation is compatible with the Convention and has called for ongoing, comprehensive review of all legislation in relation to children.

The rights of children are not always specified in national constitutions and other seminal domestic legislation – often because these documents were written long before child rights were articulated. In some countries, national legislation explicitly considers ratified international treaties such as the Convention to take precedence over domestic law. In others, particularly some of those that have written or revised their constitutions and other legal instrument since the Convention's emergence, there are specific references not just to children's care and protection but to child rights. These range from extremely detailed recognition of child rights (e.g., Brazil) to relatively brief acknowledgements (e.g., Thailand).

The Convention has been directly incorporated into national law across the world. A recent UNICEF study shows that two thirds of the 52 countries reviewed had incorporated the Convention in this way and that courts have adopted impor-

General Comments of the Committee on the Rights of the Child and general measures of implementation of the Convention

In addition to monitoring of individual countries' progress in implementing the Convention, the Committee on the Rights of the Child periodically publishes its own General Comments on key issues related to the interpretation, promotion and protection of child rights. Since 2001, the Committee has issued 12 General Comments on a wide range of topics.

General Comment No. 5: General measures of implementation:

In General Comment No. 5, the Committee on the Rights of the Child provides guidance on requisite steps that States parties must take to fulfil their obligations under the Convention. States parties, in ratifying the Convention, take on the responsibility to uphold it, but its implementation needs to engage all sectors of society, including children themselves. Key measures include:

- Developing a framework of national legislation that is fully compliant with the Convention, with rigorous and ongoing review of domestic law by government and independent bodies.
- A comprehensive national plan of action or strategy for the implementation of the Convention.
- Establishment of a permanent institution or structure within government with overall responsibility for promoting implementation and appropriate coordination between sectors and levels of government and with civil society, children and others.
- Data collection and disaggregation of data, covering the entire period of childhood up to 18.
- Child rights impact assessment and evaluation.
- Training and capacity building.
- Dissemination of information on the rights guaranteed by the Convention to children and adults alike.

GENERAL COMMENTS OF THE COMMITTEE ON THE RIGHTS OF THE CHILD

No.	Subject of the General Comment	Year of issuance
1	The aims of education	2001
2	The role of independent human rights institutions	2002
3	HIV/AIDS and the rights of the child	2003
4	Adolescent health	2003
5	General measures of implementation for the Convention on the Rights of the Child	2003
6	Treatment of unaccompanied and separated children outside their country of origin	2005
7	Implementing child rights in early childhood	2005
8	The right of the child to protection from corporal punishment and other cruel or degrading forms of punishment	2006
9	The rights of children with disabilities	2006
10	Children's rights in juvenile justice	2007
11	Indigenous children and their rights under the Convention	2009
12	The right of the child to be heard	2009

Source: General Comments are available at the website of the Committee on the Rights of the Child, <www2.ohchr.org/english/bodies/crc/comments.htm>.

- Recognition that ensuring non-discrimination may require special measures to diminish factors creating disparities.
- Meaningful consultation with children.
- Maintaining working relationships with non-governmental organizations, religious leaders, teachers, health providers, social workers, and parliamentarians.
- Budgeting for children at the national and international levels. The Committee on the Rights of the Child expects donor governments to identify the yearly amount and proportion of international aid earmarked for children's rights, and expects their programmes to be rights-based.

The Committee also strongly and continually advocates for the establishment of independent child rights institutions, including children's ombudspersons or commissioners, or for the establishment of child rights focal points within national human rights commissions or ombudspersons offices. It employs the general measures of implementation as a practical guide in making specific recommendations to States parties and expects them to describe action to take in response. Recognizing that lack of resources can hamper the full realization of economic, social, and cultural rights, the Committee emphasizes the importance of progressive realization of child rights, with the onus on States parties to implement the treaty to the maximum extent of their available resources.

See References, pages 90–92.

Providing quality education is central to enabling children to reach their full potential. *A 13-year-old boy reads aloud as his teacher and classmates listen, in Ahmet Gashi Compulsory School in Tirana, Albania.*

tant decisions applying the treaty's provisions. Furthermore, since 1989, one third of the countries studied had also integrated the Convention into their national constitutions. Almost all of these countries had made strong efforts to bring their legislation into conformity with the Convention by adopting child rights codes or through the gradual, systematic reform of existing law, or both.

This has led to some significant examples of positive change. In accordance with the principle of non-discrimination, Slovenia, for example, recognizes the right to nationality – and correspondingly, access to public services – for stateless children. Ethiopia has incorporated elements of the Convention into its 2000 family code and the amended 2004 penal code. Legislation on child protection in Indonesia and Nigeria reflects the Convention's principles. Since the Convention's emergence, many countries in Latin America, Eastern Europe and the Commonwealth of Independent States – including Belarus, Colombia, Costa Rica, the Czech Republic, Ecuador, Guatemala, Honduras, Nicaragua, Paraguay, Romania and Ukraine – have adopted new children's codes that reflect the treaty's provisions.

But integrating the Convention's principles into national legislation does not guarantee that children's rights will be realized. It is evident that in many countries the realities experienced by children do not match the rights they are guaranteed by national legislation. The success of legislation depends on

enforcement and changes in societal attitudes and practices, as well as sound principles and provisions promoting children's rights.

Many of the practices that are most harmful to children are part of social traditions and cultural attitudes that have been prevalent for generations. Simply passing a law is therefore not enough; it must be backed up with ongoing educational and awareness-raising initiatives, capacity-building, sufficient resources and collaborative partnerships, including children as full participants. This particularly applies when it comes to protecting children from violence, abuse and exploitation.

A case in point is female genital mutilation/cutting (FGM/C). Although laws against this harmful traditional practice are important, the greatest headway towards abandonment of FGM/C has been made by comprehensive campaigns that involve a community approach. Because the practice is deeply entrenched in social, economic and political structures, work towards its abandonment must involve all levels of society. Research confirms that legislation, information on the negative health consequences for women and an understanding of how the practice violates human rights, though necessary, are not sufficient for communities to abandon FGM/C. Due to social pressure to conform to community norms, even among those parents who are aware of the health risks, collective agreement to abandon the practice by a significant number of families is an essential step in this process.

The human rights-based approach to cooperation for children and women

Since 1988, UNICEF has been a leading architect and proponent of the human rights-based approach to programming to fulfil the rights of women and children under the Convention and CEDAW. The organization's country programmes are guided by human rights principles applied in all phases and sectors.

The human rights-based approach is derived from principles that underlie both conventions: accountability, universality and non-discrimination, indivisibility and participation. It is firmly embedded in the work of the United Nations, which in 2003 passed a statement of 'Common Understanding of a Human Rights-Based Approach to Development Cooperation'. Under this paradigm, an underlying aim of all UN programmes is to advance the realization of human rights as laid down in the Universal Declaration of Human Rights and other major human rights instruments.

Principles of the human rights-based approach

Universality: Human rights are innate to all people, irrespective of their ethnic origin, beliefs and practices, geographic location, gender or income level. Yet despite robust international and national legal frameworks in support of human rights, the social groups that have traditionally suffered from marginalization and discrimination within their countries and societies are still consistently the most at risk of having their rights violated or unfulfilled. A human rights-based approach specifically targets the most marginalized groups – and the most vulnerable members of these groups, which are often women and children – in the countries and communities with the greatest need.

The approach has implications for programme budgets and planning, as it is often more costly to reach marginalized groups or people living in remote rural locations or urban slums than in more mainstream areas. Immunization provides an example, where unit cost of vaccinating infants in rural areas is far higher than for their counterparts living in cities. Under a human rights-based approach to immunization, an alternative measure for determining programme priorities and allocating resources may be employed. Using the number of deaths prevented (or the healthy years gained) per immunization in place of unit costs as a determining factor in resource allocation immediately changes the cost-benefit equation, since poorer or more marginalized groups are likely to benefit most from the extension of essential services.

Innovative solutions are often required to fulfill the rights of marginalized and disadvantaged children and families. For example, the Government of India and UNICEF have partnered in an outreach initiative that has brought more than 300,000 disadvantaged children to school, using techniques such as mobile learning centres to allow hard-to-reach children access to education.

Accountability: Under a human rights-based approach, children and women are recognized as holders of rights rather than objects of charity. States parties, the signatories of the two conventions, have a duty to work towards the realization of human rights for all its citizens. The most vulnerable, notably children and women, are afforded special protection under human rights treaties and frameworks. Empowered citizens and the treaty bodies can hold governments to account for violations of human rights, and assess their progress towards implementing human rights accords. In practical terms, the human rights-based approach involves assisting all levels of the community and society to meet their obligations to children and women. In Colombia, for example, UNICEF has supported a series of policy and accountability fora in which local elected officials were questioned about their achievements and challenges in the implementation of children's rights.

Indivisibility: All human rights are indivisible and interdependent, which implies that no single right should be prioritized over another. For children, indivisibility means ensuring that the rights of the 'whole child' are met through addressing their physical, psychological, developmental and spiritual needs, and not just concentrating on the provision of essential services such as basic health care and education. It also necessitates working in partnership with other organizations with complementary skills and expertise to meet these needs. The human rights-based approach has led to greater emphasis on such broad-based concepts as early childhood development, the continuum of care for maternal, newborn and child health and a protective environment for children. It has also widened the range of core commitments to children in emergencies, including education, child protection and psychosocial therapy and counseling for those affected by natural disasters, pandemics, or armed conflict. In Viet Nam, for instance, the steady application of a human rights-based approach to development cooperation has resulted in officials developing integrated and holistic inter-sectoral policies for health, education and protection.

Participation: Central to the human rights-based approach is the premise that development cooperation is more effective when the intended end users –

both individuals and communities – participate in their planning, implementation and evaluation. Individual and community empowerment is both an object of, and a means to, the realization of human rights. Adapting programmes to the local context has been shown to be critical to their acceptance, expansion and sustainability.

For example, in Rwanda, the Government and UNICEF have supported national and local institutions in undertaking grass-roots consultations with children on the national Economic Development and Poverty Reduction Strategy. This process led to children's recommendations making their way into the final document.

Addressing disparities in child rights

The human rights-based approach to cooperation provides a holistic and integrated framework for addressing disparities in the realization of child rights. In recent years, it has become increasingly evident that the deprivations of children's rights to survival, development and certain types of protection (e.g. child labour) are largely concentrated in certain continents, regions and countries. Within nations, there are also marked disparities among children in the realization of their rights on the basis of household income, geographic location, ethnicity, gender and disability. Increasing access and providing essential services to marginalized and excluded population is critical to fulfil children's rights to survival and development.

The rights-based approach addresses disparities through identifies the most vulnerable and excluded areas and groups within countries, through with utilising of the direct, underlying causes and basic causes of the disparities they face in survival, development and protection. This approach also helps articulate the claims of the poor and marginalized through advocacy and social mobilization. It demands accountability on the part of duty bearers to fulfil the rights of women and children, and ensures that their claims are codified in national and local legislation and policies and supported by adequate budgets. It also seeks to leverage resources – financial, human, information or material – in support of policies to reduce disparities to the maximum extent possible given a country's level of development.

The Good Start in Life Program in Peru is an example of a human rights-based programme addressing the direct causes of disparities – in this case inadequate access to quality health care and information on improved nutritional and hygiene practices that contribute to high rates of stunting and micronutrient deficiency among children under three from the poorest indigenous populations in the Andean highlands and the Amazon forest of that country. The application of a cost-effective package of interventions including growth monitoring, nutritional and health care guidance to mothers, micronutrient supplementation and hygiene promotion, together with strong community involvement, helped reduce rates of stunting from 54 per cent in 2000 to 37 per cent in 2004, and decrease vitamin A deficiency from 30 per cent to around 5 per cent over the same period.

Programmes and policies also aim to address the underlying and basic causes undermining rights fulfilment. For instance, disparities in income can be addressed through poverty reduction strategies, including social protection measures such as cash transfers to poor households to support spending on social goods such as health care and education for children. Such programmes are commonly found in Latin America, with the most well-known examples being Brazil's Bolsa Escola initiative and Mexico's Oportunidades programme. But other regions are also making strides in providing income support programmes: for example, Malawi has introduced a cash transfer scheme in six districts to provide support to orphans and vulnerable children and child-headed households in particular.

Gender inequality can be addressed by increasing awareness of discriminatory practices and promoting legal and social reforms. Disparities in the provision of essential services due to geographical location can be reduced by applying integrated services and mobile services. For example, in southern Sudan, child immunization programmes have been successfully combined with cattle vaccination against rinderpest. Expanding educational opportunities to mothers is pivotal to improving children's survival and development, as research has shown that educated women are less likely to die in childbirth and are more likely to send their children to school.

A key challenge ahead is to monitor and evaluate the effectiveness of human rights-based programmes, not only in producing better outcomes for child survival, development, protection and participation but also in transforming attitudes, practices, policies, laws and programmes that support the fulfilment of children's rights.

See References, pages 90–92.

Child rights in South Africa

Twenty years ago, South Africa was just beginning to loosen the grip of apartheid, and many children suffered rights violations – including assault, torture, detention without trial, and restricted access to health care, education and protection. Institutional segregation was dismantled through negotiations between 1990 and 1993, and a new constitution was instituted in 1996. On 22 April 2009, the country completed its fourth consecutive democratic election.

Child rights at the heart of the post-apartheid constitution

After ratifying the Convention on the Rights of the Child on 16 July 1995, the architects of the new South Africa embedded its precepts into their country's constitution. Section 28 of South Africa's Bill of Rights guarantees children's right to an identity, basic services, education and protection within the legal system. Other key legislation to protect the rights of children introduced during the post-apartheid era includes the Films and Publications Act, the Basic Conditions of Employment Act, the Domestic Violence Act, the Child Justice Act and the Sexual Offences Act.

The most comprehensive addition to the child rights framework is the 2005 Children's Act and Amendment, which reinforces provisions in the Bill of Rights and details the responsibilities of parents and guardians. Important provisions include the right of access to state grants for children over age 16 who head households, and greater access to health care for young people, including the right of consent to HIV testing and treatment.

The challenges of enacting child rights

This strong framework is necessary, but not sufficient, for ensuring that children are protected and have the scope to participate as empowered citizens. Reversing decades of social problems fostered by apartheid is challenging, particularly in the face of widespread poverty, the recent global economic downturn, and the national and regional AIDS pandemic.

More than one quarter of the population is living on less than US$1.25 per day, according to the most recent international estimates, and the country's income distribution is among the most unequal in the world. In 2007, around 18 per cent of adults aged 15–49 were HIV-positive. Among the country's youth, 4 per cent of males and 13 per cent of females aged 15–24 were living with HIV. An estimated 1.4 million children under 18, or 8 per cent of South Africa's children, have lost one or both parents to AIDS.

Confronting the task ahead

The Government of South Africa faces the challenge of accelerating progress on survival, development, protection and participation for the country's 18 million children. Some essential services have relatively high levels of coverage by international standards. For example, coverage of routine immunization as measured by three doses of diphtheria, pertussis and tetanus toxoid vaccine stands at 97 per cent, while 93 per cent of the population – and 100 per cent in urban areas – has access to improved drinking water.

In other areas, faster progress is required. The latest international estimates indicate that 14 per cent of primary-school-age children are not enrolled in the appropriate education level; at the secondary level, 30 per cent of adolescent boys and 25 per cent of girls from the typical age cohort for secondary education are not enrolled. Sanitation facilities are sorely lacking, with more than one third of urban dwellers and more than half of rural residents still living without access to improved sanitation facilities.

Fighting the AIDS pandemic and alleviating the associated effects on children is another high priority. Substantial progress is being made, from prevention to treatment. But given the scale of the pandemic, with 5.7 million people living with HIV in 2007, greater efforts at all levels are urgently required. Violence against children remains at high levels, despite provisions embodied in the Children's Act. And around 22 per cent of South African children are not registered at birth. Birth registration facilitates children's access to basic services, including child support grants.

In South Africa, children have been energetic participants in defence of their rights. In 1992, for example, the Molo Songololo organization hosted a summit on child rights attended by hundreds of children. Their collective vision was adopted into the Children's Charter of South Africa. Children and young people also participated in the drafting of the 2005 Children's Act, which has child participation as one of its founding principles.

The South African Parliament and Government, at national and local levels, are working to raise children's and parents' awareness about their rights. And the rights of children and women are nationally recognized in a comprehensive framework that provides a firm foundation for their fulfilment. Bridging the gap between rights and meeting the obligations to realize them is the next step.

See References, pages 90–92.

The impact of the Convention on child survival and development, protection and participation

For a broader picture of the progress of nations in guaranteeing child rights, it is necessary to examine evidence on and indicators related to the rights stated in the Convention. In this report, these rights are examined in three main categories: survival and development; protection; and participation.

Survival and development includes basic health and health care, disease prevention and control, nutrition, water supply, sanitation and environmental health; early learning and stimulation, education, leisure and cultural activities; and family guidance and care. Considerable achievements have been made in this area of child rights during the past 20 years, although much remains to be done.

Protection involves safeguarding children from risks to their mental, physical and emotional well-being, including emergency situations, conflict with the law, violence, abuse, exploitation, neglect and discrimination. Although notable advances have been made in this area, they can be difficult to quantify, owing, in part, to considerable gaps in the data on child protection abuses and the lack of implementation of civil rights for children.

Participation promotes the empowerment and capacity of children to be involved in the decisions and actions that affect them. It examines issues related to civil rights and freedoms including freedom of expression, thought, conscience and religion, association and peaceful assembly, the right to information and children's right to express their views in matters affecting them.

Wherever possible, key indicators will be employed to measure progress between 1990, the reference year for the Millennium Development Goals and the year in which the Convention came into force, and the latest year for which data are available. Areas for which trend data are not available at the global level or are not sufficiently reliable will be addressed through a qualitative description of progress and challenges.

SURVIVAL AND DEVELOPMENT

Marked progress in child survival, disease control and education

At the global level, there has been substantial progress since 1990 in key survival and development outcomes and in provid-ing of essential services, enhanced utilization of healthy behaviours and practices, and diminished gender discrimination in access to education. Advances in these areas have been most notable in three developing regions: Central and Eastern Europe and the Commonwealth of Independent States (CEE/CIS), East Asia, and Latin America and the Caribbean. Many countries in the Middle East and North Africa, and several in South Asia and sub-Saharan Africa, have also experienced substantial gains in child survival, health and education.

Child survival has long been championed by UNICEF and other child rights organization as a benchmark indicator for child development because it reflects many other inputs that determine child rights: maternal health and nutritional status, equality and empowerment for women and girls, access to basic and maternity health services, education, environmental health and income. By this standard, progress has been significant, with the number of deaths among children under 5 years old reduced from 12.5 million in 1990 to less than 9 million in 2008, the most recent year for which data were available at the time of publication. Correspondingly, the rate of under-five mortality fell from 90 deaths per 1,000 live births to 65 deaths per 1,000 live births over the same period.

Fewer child deaths reflect, in part, the success of national governments and the international health community in combating several major childhood diseases, largely through expanded immunization programmes. Polio, which causes disability and morbidity among children, is close to eradication, despite pockets of resistance. Between 2000 and 2007, child deaths from measles declined by 74 per cent globally, and by a remarkable 89 per cent in Africa. Millions of lives have been saved through immunization against diphtheria, pertussis, tetanus, hepatitis and other vaccine-preventable diseases and conditions.

There has also been evidence of declining HIV prevalence rates. In 14 of 17 African countries with adequate survey data, the percentage of pregnant women 15–24 years old living with HIV has declined since 2000/2001. In seven countries, the drop in rates of HIV infection has equalled or exceeded the 25 per cent targeted reduction for 2010 set out in the Declaration of Commitment on HIV/AIDS adopted at the 2001 UN General Assembly Special Session on HIV and AIDS. In addition, more pregnant women than ever before have access to and use services to prevent transmission of HIV to their babies.

Other child development outcomes have also seen progress. Undernutrition, as measured by underweight prevalence among under-fives in developing countries, has declined in all develop-

Progress on survival and development rights

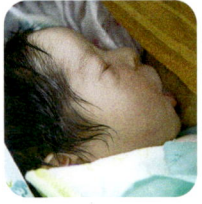
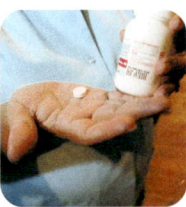
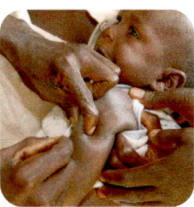
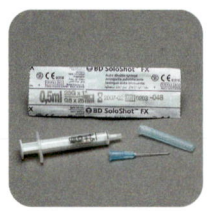
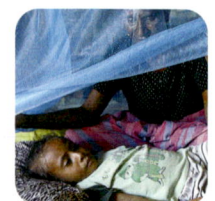

Child survival
The annual number of global under-five deaths has dropped from 12.5 million in 1990 to less than 9 million in 2008.

Exclusive breastfeeding
for infants less than six months old has increased in all but one developing region.

Micronutrient supplementation
fully protecting children in developing regions with two doses of vitamin A has risen from 16% to 62% since 1999.

Routine immunization
of three doses of DPT3 vaccine has increased from 75% in 1990 to 81% in 2007.

Vaccines
save millions of lives and have helped reduce global measles deaths by 74% since 2000.

Malaria prevention
Use of insecticide-treated mosquito nets for under-fives has risen sharply in sub-Saharan Africa since 2000.

ing regions since 1990. The number of children out of primary school was reduced from 115 million in 2002 to 101 million in 2007, and around 84 per cent of children of the appropriate age are now in primary school. Recent estimates suggest that on any given day, more than 1 billion school-age children are accessing primary or secondary education. The latest survey data indicate that around 90 per cent of children entering primary school remain in school until the final grade. In addition, global and regional gender gaps in primary education have generally closed, leaving the gender parity index at 96 per cent for developing countries – although regional and country variations are marked, and girls remain at greater risk than boys of missing out on primary education.

Stronger advances are required in many areas of child development

Alongside these results, however, there is ample evidence that major challenges remain in realizing children's rights to health care, nutrition, education and family care and protection. Even in areas where gains have been made, there is still much work to be done, as the photo panel on pages 18–19 attests. In child survival, which shows perhaps the most measurable advance, an average of 25,000 children under five are still dying each day, mostly from causes preventable with low-cost, proven interventions. A 2003 study on child poverty by the London School of Economics and the University of Bristol on behalf of UNICEF revealed that more than 1 billion children are deprived of at least one of their rights in education, water and sanitation, access to information, essential health care, nutrition and shelter.

There are some areas of child survival and development where advances have been limited or are overshadowed by the extent of continued deprivation. This is particularly true for maternal survival, as the annual burden of maternal deaths has remained intractable at around 500,000 since 1990. Despite expanded access to maternity services in several developing regions, the latest international estimates indicate that roughly 1 in every 4 pregnant women does not receive even a single antenatal care visit from a skilled health professional, and 2 of every 5 deliveries occur without the

SURVIVAL AND DEVELOPMENT RIGHTS

According to the Convention on the Rights of the Child, every child has the right to:

	ARTICLES
Family relations and parental guidance	5, 8, 9, 10,18, 21, 25
Life, survival and development	6
Registration, name, nationality, care and preservation of identity	7, 8
Access to appropriate information	13, 17
Health and access to health-care services	24
Benefit from social security	26
A decent standard of living	27
Education	28, 29

Source: Derived from the Convention on the Rights of the Child.

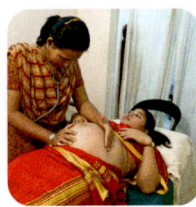

HIV prevalence

has declined among women aged 15–24 attending antenatal clinics since 2000, in 14 of 17 countries with sufficient data to determine trends.

HIV treatment

for children under 15 has risen dramatically, most significantly in sub-Saharan Africa.

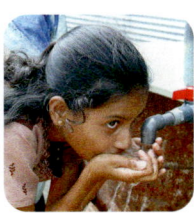

Improved drinking water

More than 1.6 billion people have gained access to improved drinking-water sources between 1990 and 2006.

Primary school enrolment

The number of children out of school declined from 115 million in 2002 to 101 million in 2007.

Primary school completion

Survival to the last primary grade for children in developing countries was more than 90% in 2000-2007 according to international survey data.

Gender parity in primary education

is improving, with the gender parity index at 96% or higher in most developing regions.

assistance of a doctor, nurse or midwife. A related issue is low birthweight – around 14 per cent of children are born weighing less than 2,500 grams – a condition that often derives from the mother's poor health and nutritional status. Inadequate health care and nutrition for women also contribute to high numbers of neonatal deaths, with 4 million newborns dying within the first month after birth each year.

Pneumonia and diarrhoeal diseases are the biggest killers of children under five, accounting for almost 40 per cent of deaths for this age cohort. Yet access to antibiotics and oral rehydration therapy – simple, proven interventions to combat these diseases and conditions – remains low in many developing countries. In South Asia, only 18 per cent of under-fives with suspected pneumonia are receiving antibiotics; in sub-Saharan Africa, less than one third of under-fives with diarrhoea receive the recommended treatment – oral rehydration with continued feeding. Sanitation, which is critical to safeguarding against infection and undernutrition, is another area that urgently requires greater attention. Although global sanitation coverage has increased from 54 per cent in 1990 to 62 per cent in 2006, almost half of the developing world's population continues to live without access to improved sanitation facilities.

Although sustained and substantial investments in HIV prevention and treatment are lowering the rate of new infections and expanding access to antiretroviral therapy, the demand for testing, treatment and effective prevention interventions such as life skills education continues to outstrip supply. More than 30 million people 15–49 years old are living with HIV across the world,

as are 2 million children aged 14 or younger. Children's rights to survival, development and health are constantly challenged in resource-poor environments and where health and social protection systems are underdeveloped or malfunctioning.

In education, too, challenges abound. Through its General Comment No. 7, the Committee on the Rights of the Child has placed a strong emphasis on early learning for children prior to primary school. It is estimated that due to poverty and the resulting lack of stimulation, an estimated 200 million children under five are at risk of not developing to their full potential. Early childhood development is an important foundation for primary school achievement and quality learning. Children from poor households would benefit greatly from early childhood development programmes but are among those with the least access to such initiatives.

Gains in primary school enrolment and completion are not being replicated at the secondary level, with only 42 per cent of children of appropriate age in the developing world (excluding China) attending secondary school. Higher enrolment in primary education is also leading to concerns that educational quality needs to keep pace to ensure that children completing primary school have a strong foundation for further learning.

Greater efforts needed to confront widening disparities

It has become increasingly apparent during recent years that the deprivations of child rights to survival and development

Challenges of survival and development

  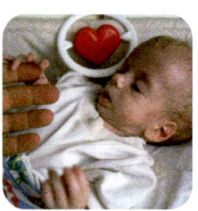  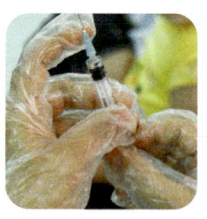 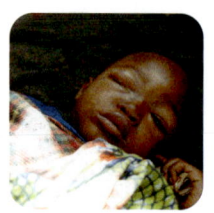

2.5 billion

people still lack access to improved sanitation facilities.

1 billion

children are deprived of one or more services essential to survival and development.

148 million

under-fives in developing regions are underweight for their age.

101 million

children are not attending primary school, with more girls than boys missing out.

22 million

infants are not protected from diseases by routine immunization.

8.8 million

children worldwide died before their fifth birthday in 2008.

are concentrated in certain continents, regions and countries. Within countries, the communities, social and population groups that experience marginalization, severe impoverishment or discrimination are also those most likely to experience higher rates of child mortality and poorer development outcomes.

Several key factors are associated with a greater likelihood of children being deprived of their right to essential services:

Continent and region – Africa and Asia present the largest global challenges for survival, development and protection. At the regional level, sub-Saharan Africa and South Asia are well behind all other regions on most indicators. These are, for example, the only regions where the under-five mortality rate exceeded 50 per 1,000 live births in 2008, with South Asia at 76 and sub-Saharan Africa at 144. The rate of child marriage is also much higher in these two regions than any other, at 46 per cent for South Asia and 39 per cent for sub-Saharan Africa; moreover, the births of 2 out of every 3 children go unregistered.[6]

Gender – In 2007, of the estimated 101 million children of appropriate age not attending primary school, the majority were girls.[7] The largest gender gaps at the primary level are in West and Central Africa, the Middle East and North Africa, and South Asia. Girls from poor and rural households are particularly at risk of missing out on primary and secondary education. Gender gaps in access to health care are also apparent in some countries of South Asia and sub-Saharan Africa. Besides being a violation of norms and laws in its own right, child marriage, which mostly involves girls, heightens the risk

of girls missing out on an education and becoming pregnant in adolescence, with attendant health risks to both the mother and the child. Young women continue to be disproportionately vulnerable to HIV infection in Eastern and Southern Africa, with adolescent girls around 2 to 4.5 times more likely to be living with HIV than their male counterparts.[8]

Household income – Children of income-poor families have far higher rates of under-five mortality and are less likely to be in school than children from wealthier families. The primary school net attendance ratio in 2000–2006 was 65 per cent for children from the poorest fifth of households in developing countries, compared with 88 per cent for children from the richest households. Children from poorer households are also much more likely to be engaged in child labour than those from richer households – in both Bolivia and Nicaragua, for example, children in the poorest quintile are 6 times as likely to engage in child labour as those in the richest quintile.[9]

Urban/rural divide – Across all developing regions and almost all aspects of primary health care and education, children living in urban areas are more likely to have access to essential services and commodities than those living in rural areas. This is particularly notable in measures of environmental health; in 2006, for example, only 45 per cent of the world's rural population had access to basic sanitation facilities, compared with 79 per cent in urban areas.

Mother's education – Along with her own health and well-being, a mother's level of education has a strong influence on the likelihood that her children will survive until age five and beyond, receive adequate nourishment and attend school. A

co-operation" with regard to the cultural, economic and social rights of children. Targeting services to reach those children most affected by disparities, a key principle of the human rights-based approach to cooperation (*see panel, pages 12–13*) will be even more necessary in these difficult times, because their families and communities may be hard hit by the global economic recession and lower inflows of aid and remittances. International cooperation, too, must be sustained to ensure that children's right to essential services and commodities is ensured during the crisis period and beyond.

Delivering essential services for children

For those children who are denied survival and development, expanding coverage of essential services will be critical to fulfilling their rights. 'Going to scale' involves a complex range of actions, including expanding the delivery of proven interventions and overcoming behavioural, institutional and environmental impediments to service delivery; all require a good understanding of the bottlenecks to delivering essential services for children. Effective scale-up also requires enhanced collaboration between stakeholders. Initiatives and partnerships directed towards meeting children's right to survival and development are numerous and continue to proliferate, but without greater coherence and harmonization, these efforts risk falling short of their intended targets.

Many of the solutions for scaling up service delivery are derived from the field of primary health care, but they are equally applicable to education and other areas of child survival and development such as appropriate information and adequate shelter. These solutions include:

- Ensuring that children's rights to survival and development are a central objective of integrated national strategies for expanding and improving the quality of essential services;
- Improving the quality and consistency of financing;
- Encouraging and sustaining political commitment to, and national and international leadership for, enhanced and expanded service delivery;
- Creating the conditions for greater harmonization between global initiatives and partnerships, and with national agencies;
- Strengthening infrastructure, transportation, logistics, supplies and training of professionals entrusted with children's health care and education;
- Improving the quality of data collection and analysis; and
- Empowering children and families to demand their right to essential services.

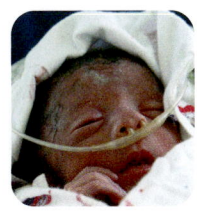

4 million

newborns worldwide are dying in the first month of life.

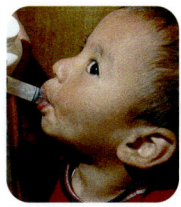

2 million

children under 15 worldwide are living with HIV.

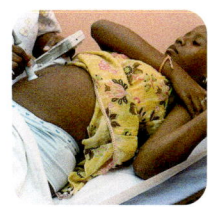

>500,000

women die each year from causes related to pregnancy and childbirth.

2005 UNICEF study of primary school attendance in 18 African countries showed 73 per cent of children of educated mothers attending compared with 51 per cent of children of uneducated mothers.

Disability – Although the Convention specifies that the State is responsible for providing special care and protection for children living with disabilities, emerging evidence indicates these children are more likely to miss out on essential services and suffer higher risks of protection abuses than other children. Children with disabilities often suffer discrimination and exclusion and are particularly vulnerable to physical violence as well as sexual, emotional and verbal abuse. They are also less likely to be in school.[10]

Minority or indigenous status – Of growing concern during recent years is the increasing evidence of disparities based on ethnicity, with numerous studies indicating widespread neglect of the rights of children among minority and indigenous populations. Although birth registration rates in Latin America and the Caribbean, for example, are far higher than in most other developing regions, they are much lower for children from indigenous minorities within the region.[11]

The global food, fuel and financial crises that erupted in 2008, leading to a worldwide recession and tightening national budgets in 2009, have raised concerns that disparities in access to essential services will further prevent children from realizing their right to survival and development. According to article 4 of the Convention, States parties should "undertake measures to the maximum possible extent of their available resources and, where needed, within the framework of international

Challenges of disparities

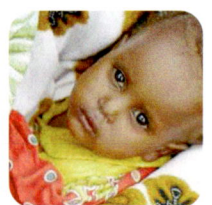 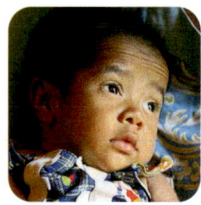 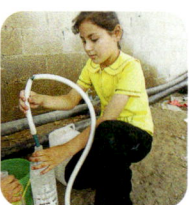   

Child mortality

Child mortality among the poor is at least 1.9 times higher than among the rich in more than half of 90 countries with sufficient data to make an assessment.

Underweight prevalence

is more than twice as likely for under-fives who are poor than for those who are rich in developing countries.

Piped drinking-water connections

are more than twice as accessible for urban households than for rural ones.

Improved sanitation facilities

are almost twice as accessible for urban dwellers than for rural ones in developing countries.

HIV prevalence

among young women in Eastern and Southern Africa is 3 times higher than among young men.

Comprehensive knowledge of HIV

among young men in South Asia is twice the rate of young women.

Establishing continua of maternal, newborn and child primary health care

The continuum of care entails delivering essential care at critical points in the life cycle and at pivotal locations. Essential services for mothers, newborns and children are most effective when they are delivered in integrated packages and delivery systems, underpinned by an environment that supports the rights of women and girls. The essential services required to support a continuum of care entail enhanced nutrition; safe water, sanitation and hygiene facilities and practices; disease prevention, testing, treatment and follow-up; quality reproductive health services – including adequate antenatal and post-natal care, skilled assistance at delivery, and comprehensive emergency obstetric and newborn care; and Integrated Management of Neonatal and Childhood Illnesses.

Establishing effective continua of care will involve taking practical steps to strengthen primary health care systems. Given the particular challenges, risks and opportunities associated with pregnancy, childbirth and early childhood, these areas require more focused attention.

Make education systems child-friendly

Realizing child rights will require getting the millions of children still missing out on primary and secondary education, who are mostly girls, into school. The challenge also extends to improving the overall quality of schooling and addressing threats to participation. Enhanced access and quality will have multiplier effects, enabling enrolled children to have higher rates of attendance and completion, better learning outcomes, and increasing rates of transition to the next level of education and to meaningful employment.

Quality education implies ensuring that schools work in the best interests of the children. This means providing safe and protective schools that are adequately staffed with trained teachers, equipped with adequate resources and graced with appropriate conditions for learning. Recognizing that different children face different circumstances and have different needs, such schools build on the assets children bring from their homes and communities, and also compensate for shortcomings in the home or community environment. They enable children to achieve, at a minimum, the knowledge and skills prescribed in the curriculum. They also help them develop the ability to think and reason, build self-respect and respect for others, and reach their full potential as individuals, members of their communities and citizens of the world. This, in turn, equips them to claim their rights, and also to contribute to realizing the rights of others. Child-friendly schools embrace a multidimensional concept of quality and address the total needs of the child as a learner.

PROTECTION

Prior to the adoption of the Convention, efforts to protect children from violence, abuse, exploitation, neglect and dis-

Youth literacy

among young men is 1.2 times higher than among young women in the least developed countries.

Net secondary school attendance

in Latin America and the Caribbean for boys is 6 percentage points lower than for girls.

Child marriage

among young women living in rural areas of the developing world is twice that of young women from cities.

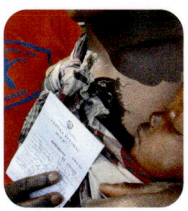

Birth registration

is almost twice as likely for children born in cities than those born in rural areas.

Attendance of skilled health personnel at delivery

for women from the richest income quintile in developing countries is 2 times higher than for the poorest developing countries.

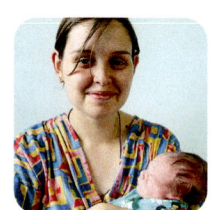

Lifetime risk of maternal death

is 300 times greater for women living in the least developed countries than it is for those from industrialized countries.

crimination were largely addressed by issue-specific initiatives, such as those to standardize the legal age of marriage. An important exception to this was children affected by armed conflict, where multiple, collaborative efforts were undertaken to protect children from the full range of threats to their survival, development, protection and participation posed by wars that were increasingly affecting civilian populations. Issue-specific initiatives remain a core component of child protection today. However, as the 20th century progressed, there were growing concerns about what was described by UNICEF in the mid-1980s and 1990s as 'children in especially difficult circumstances' – homeless, orphaned, living and working on the streets, affected by conflict and disabilities, or suffering from violence, abuse, exploitation and neglect. It was increasingly understood that these children faced a range of rights violations that would be best served dealing with as a whole.

The Convention paved the way for the consolidation of child protection as a holistic concept. It offers children a protective environment from a broad spectrum of violence, discrimination and exploitation, because all children – whether from industrialized countries or developing countries, from rich or poor communities, in situations of peace and security or conflict and emergency – need protection from neglect and abuse.

Children's right to protection is further enhanced by two Optional Protocols added to the Convention in 2000: on the Sale of Children, Child Prostitution and Child Pornography,

and on the Involvement of Children in Armed Conflict. Other international human rights instruments also elaborate and strengthen children's right to protection. Among these are CEDAW; the International Labour Organization's conventions on the minimum age for admission to employment (no. 138) and on elimination of the worst forms of child labour (no. 182); the Protocol to Prevent, Suppress and Punish Trafficking in Persons, especially Women and Children supplementing the UN Convention against Transnational Organized Crime; the Hague Convention on Protection of Children and Cooperation in Respect of Intercountry Adoption; and the Convention on the Rights of Persons with Disabilities.

Protection risks for children are numerous and complex

Children suffer from violence, abuse, exploitation, neglect and discrimination in every country and community, cultural, social or economic group. These violations are under-recognized and under-reported barriers to child rights, and undermine survival, development and participation. Both the physical and psychological effects of child protection abuses can be marked, leading to lifelong consequences and profound difficulties. Child protection violations are also associated with, and are often a cause or consequence of, discrimination, poverty, and the denial of children's rights to essential goods and services, a decent standard of living, family environment, identity and other civil, social and economic freedoms.

Child rights in China

With 1.33 billion people in 2007, China holds one fifth of the global population – including 342 million children, most of them living in rural areas.

China ratified the Convention in March 1992, the Optional Protocol on the Sale of Children, Child Prostitution and Child Pornography in December 2002, and the Optional Protocol on the Involvement of Children in Armed Conflict in December 2007. It has ratified many international accords on child rights and has a strong body of domestic legislation on the promotion and protection of a wide range of child rights.

During the past two decades, child survival and development in China have steadily improved. According to the latest UN inter-agency statistics, the under-five mortality rate was reduced by 51 per cent between 1990 and 2007. An estimated 94 per cent of infants receive routine immunization, as measured by coverage of infants receiving three doses of diphtheria, pertussis and tetanus toxoid vaccine. And, at 3.7 per cent in 2003, the percentage of infants with low birthweight is among the lowest in the world.

Some disparities remain amid remarkable poverty reduction

The economic transformation that began in 1978 allowed GDP per capita to grow at an average annual rate of 9 per cent in 1990–2007. This has generated a remarkable reduction in poverty: Between 1981 and 2004, the proportion of the population who live on less than US$1.25 a day was reduced from 85 per cent to 27 per cent, and more than half a billion people escaped absolute poverty.

In general, China's children are benefiting from lower material deprivation and better access to quality health care and education. Enrolment in primary school,

for example, is nearly universal for both girls and boys. But as in other middle-income countries, economic advances have been uneven, exacerbating disparities among diverse geographical and income groups. Infant mortality rates, for example, are almost five times higher in the most impoverished districts than in the wealthiest provinces. Similarly, under-five mortality rates for the lowest socio-economic quintile by area of residence are six times higher than those of the wealthiest group.

These disparities are compounded by limited access to quality health services for those living in poor and rural areas as well as those who are part of a massive population movement. China has an estimated 150 million internal migrants, accounting for more than 11 per cent of its population. Among those who have migrated within the country, an estimated 25 million are under age 18, and 58 million children have been left behind in rural areas as their parents seek work in the cities.

A traditional preference for boys has resulted in a significant increase in the sex-ratio imbalance since the 1980s. Data for 2005 show a sex ratio at birth of 119 boys to every 100 girls, rising from 109 in 1982. Although policies have been implemented to address this issue, further action, particularly in the area of social protection, is required to reduce the dependence of rural parents on their sons for support in old age, sickness and other difficulties.

Committing to social development that will sustain child protection

In 2006, the Government of China adopted a new resolution on building a sustainable and harmonious society, with children included as a main concern in the social development process. The resolution is incorporated in the

11th Five-Year Plan (2006–2010), adopted by the National People's Congress in March 2006. The plan also reaffirmed the Government's commitment to the 2001–2010 National Plan of Action for Children and Women's Development. Among the efforts to strengthen public services, the national 'Building a New Socialist Countryside' initiative commits the Government to providing free compulsory basic education and reforming the public social security system.

Challenges ahead

China faces the challenge of consolidating its gains in child rights and ensuring that growth is accompanied by diminishing disparities. In particular, it faces the task of meeting the material and protection needs of rural children, children affected by migration, and those living in the poor areas that are rapidly expanding around the major conurbations.

As an emerging international donor to other developing nations, and a major actor in the international economy, China has an unprecedented opportunity to support and promote child rights beyond its borders. Investing in child rights is among the surest ways to ensure that China's economic and social progress is both consolidated and deepened in years to come.

See References, pages 90–92.

Child rights in Egypt

The world's largest Arab nation, Egypt had an estimated 75 million inhabitants in 2007, an estimated 39 per cent of them under 18. Its landscape is dominated by the Nile Valley, the Nile Delta and the desert. Just 5 per cent of its geographical area is fit for human settlement.

One of six countries to convene the World Summit for Children in 1990, Egypt ratified the Convention in September of that year. Since then, it has achieved outstanding gains in the areas of health and education through ample government investment.

Considerable progress in child survival and development

Between 1992 and 2008, the under-five mortality rate declined by two thirds, falling from 85 to 28 deaths per 1,000 live births over the period. Neonatal mortality dropped by one half between 1992 and 2008; maternal mortality declined to 130 deaths per 100,000 live births, largely owing to rising antenatal care coverage and skilled health personnel attending births.

Public campaigns to promote the use of oral rehydration salts have lowered infant mortality associated with diarrhoeal diseases, once among the most serious threats to child survival, while routine immunization reached 98 per cent by 2007.

Although progress in gender parity in education has been slower than other child development indicators, ratios of girls to boys in primary and secondary schools have shown some improvement.

Disparities remain wide

At the national level, Egypt is on track to achieve most of the Millennium Development Goals. The provincial level, however, is marked by increasing disparities. The Egyptian Government's histori-cally centralized approach to welfare provision has not always prioritized extending programmes to rural and remote populations. Upper Egypt, home to more than one third of the country's population, lags behind Lower Egypt in income and social development indicators. Between 2005 and 2008, while poverty declined by 20 per cent national-ly, the reduction in rural Upper Egypt was around one third of the national average. By 2008, poverty in rural Upper Egypt was as high as 40 per cent, more than twice the national average.

In the sparsely populated areas of northern Egypt, some communities lack access to schools, health care and water. Bedouin children of South Sinai have a high incidence of wasting, stunt-ing and urinary tract infections, all three preventable with basic preventive and curative measures.

Disparities among girls are consider-able, depending on their geographical residence and parents' level of educa-tion, among other factors. In Upper Egypt, for example, the incidence of female genital mutilation/cutting (FGM/C) exceeds 85 per cent, while in private urban schools the rate dips below 10 per cent. According to the 2008 Egypt Demographic and Health Survey, 24 per cent of girls under 18 have undergone female genital mutila-tion, with rates rising to 75 per cent among girls aged 15–17 years.

In 2008, following the death of a 12-year-old girl undergoing genital cutting the previous year, the Government amended the 1997 child protection law, banning FGM/C and reinforcing the ban with fines and imprisonment for any breaches. The practice continues despite the ban, but it has noticeably declined, mostly as a result of public education campaigns.

In addition to banning FGM/C, Egypt's child protection law prevents children in conflict with the law from being tried on the same basis as adults, ensures birth certificates for children of unwed mothers, restricts corporal punishment and raises the earliest age for marriage to 18. Implementation of this protective legislation has brought child and youth issues to the forefront, generating intense debate among conservative Islamists, moderates and secularists about the role of state, religion and families in child welfare.

In one area – water supply – Egypt faces a grave threat to both human and child development. According to the United Nations Development Programme's *Egypt Human Development Report 2008,*" One of the greatest challenges facing Egypt today is the number of rural and urban households in need of basic infrastructure (mainly water supply and sewage)". As part of its 2007–2012 national development plan, the Government of Egypt has set aside approximately \$13 billion to expand water supply service for all Egyptians, but even with this massive investment, it is estimated that only 40 per cent of Egyptian villages will have a sewage system.

Challenges ahead

Egypt has many successful past experi-ences on which to base future pro-grammes to meet the needs of all its citizens, especially children and young people. The country still confronts many challenges – particularly in addressing disparities and strengthening child pro-tection. Reaching children in remote and rural areas will remain a key challenge for the Government in its attempts to fulfil the rights of all children. Further progress on child rights will also require greater inclusion of all domestic stakeholders, as well as strong international cooperation.

See References, pages 90–92.

Challenges of protection

     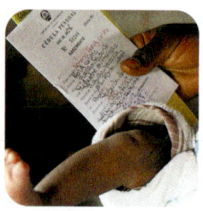

500 million–1.5 billion
children have been affected by violence.

150 million
children 5–14 years old are engaged in child labour.

145 million
children have lost one or both parents due to all causes.

70 million
women and girls in 29 countries have experienced female genital mutilation/cutting.

> 64 million
women aged 20–24 in the developing world reported they were married before age 18.

51 million
children are unregistered at birth.

Most child protection violations are hard to measure and monitor, owing to both social norms that condone these practices and political sensitivities related to such issues as child labour, sexual exploitation and corporal punishment but also due to gaps in defining, collecting and analysing appropriate indicators to measure protection abuses. In addition, given that the perpetrators of many abuses against children often go to great lengths to hide their deeds, and the shame and stigma attached to violations that foster under-reporting in all societies, it is hard to accurately assess the scale of child protection violations. In many cases, children are afraid to report incidents of violence, abuse and exploitation against them.

Since the mid-1980s, international household surveys such as the Demographic and Health Surveys (DHS) and Multiple Indicator Cluster Surveys (MICS), along with improved national monitoring, have helped bring child protection into sharper focus by providing regular estimates for key indicators. The key protection indicators measured include birth registration, child marriage, child labour, female genital mutilation/cutting and, more recently, attitudes towards domestic violence, child discipline and child disability. Both the data collection process and the resultant estimates are still works in progress, and the numbers presented in the photo panel on pages 24–25 are therefore only a rough and partial representation of the scope of violations against children's right to protection. These estimates derive from another UNICEF flagship publication: *Progress for Children: A report card on child protection*, also published in 2009.

The latest estimates derived from international household surveys present an alarming array of violations of children's right to protection from harm and denial of civil freedoms –

such as the right to an identity – across the developing world. Violence may affect between 500 million and 1.5 billion children, and an estimated 150 million children aged 5–14 are engaged in child labour. More than 70 million women and girls aged 15–49 in 29 countries have been subjected to female genital mutilation/cutting.

Although birth registration is fundamental to the realization of child rights, legitimizing the existence of a child's life while simultaneously recording the State's recognition of the child as a citizen, more than 50 million children are not registered at birth. More than 64 million women aged 20–24 in the developing world were married or in union before age 18. More than 1 billion children are estimated to live in countries or territories affected by armed conflict; of these, around 300 million are under age five. Although there is evidence of some progress – declining incidence of FGM/C – the pace of these improvements is slow.

Similar factors that undermine children's right to survival and development also heighten the risk of protection violations. Extreme poverty is associated with higher levels of child marriage, child labour and exploitation. The risks for HIV infection among girls and women are likely to increase where poverty is greatest. Recent studies in five countries in Southern Africa (Botswana, Malawi, Swaziland, the United Republic of Tanzania and Zambia) have shown the links between acute food insecurity and unprotected transactional sex among poor women.[12] Children in conflict-affected countries may face increased risks of being exploited, exposure to violence or being recruited by armed groups. When civil strife and extreme poverty coincide, as they do in conflict-affected countries of West and Central Africa such as the Democratic

18 million

children are living with the effects of displacement.

15 million

children have lost one or both parents due to AIDS.

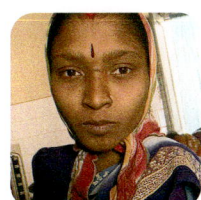

14 million

young women give birth between the ages of 15 and 19 years old.

1.2 million

children were trafficked each year as of the year 2000.

>1 million

children are detained through justice processes.

Republic of the Congo, children are susceptible to a much higher risk of child protection violations.

Disparities in child protection are also apparent within countries and broadly correlate with the same causal factors as those for survival and development: region or continent, geographical location, ethnicity, disability, gender and income. For example, children from the poorest households are twice as likely to be unregistered at birth as those from the richest families. A girl from a rural household in the developing countries of Eastern and Southern Africa is twice as likely to be married before age 18 as her urban counterpart. Studies show that girls in rural areas are engaged in agricultural labour at an earlier age than boys, and they are more often abused and exploited, although boys are also affected.

Violence, child labour and trafficking are also of particular concern in industrialized countries. A recent review of studies on child maltreatment published in *The Lancet* reveals that at least 4 per cent of children in industrialized countries are physically abused each year, and 1 in every 10 is neglected or psychologically abused. It is estimated that 5–10 per cent of girls and up to 5 per cent of boys suffer penetrative sexual abuse over the course of their childhood; the percentage of children experiencing any form of sexual abuse could be as much as three times higher. Abused children are at greater risk of experiencing a range of difficulties, including mental health issues, low education achievement, substance abuse, relationship problems and perpetrating violence later in life.

Migrant children, particularly those belonging to families without documentation or who have migrated illegally, may be at greater risk of exploitation such as trafficking. Lacking support services, children of immigrants and other marginalized populations may be less likely to be registered at birth or to have access to essential services and legal recourse to justice to protect their rights. Children who are vulnerable to protection violations may also experience responses and actions that exacerbate these threats. Children who come into conflict with the law also face protection risks, particularly violence, at every stage of contact with justice systems. Child victims of and witnesses to human-rights abuses often lack the support of skilled professionals and sensitive procedures

PROTECTION RIGHTS

According to the Convention on the Rights of the Child, every child has the right to protection from:

	ARTICLES
Illicit transfers and illegal adoption	11,21
Violence, abuse, exploitation and neglect	19
Armed conflict	22, 38-39
Child labour, trafficking, sexual and other forms of exploitation, and drug abuse	32-36,39
Torture and deprivation of liberty, and capital punishment	37-39

In addition, the Convention assures special protection, assistance and care for children who are :

Deprived of the family environment	20,22
Disabled	23
In conflict with the law	37, 39–40

Source: Derived from the Convention on the Rights of the Child.

The Convention's impact on public and private institutions

The Convention's impact on public and private institutions, including all three branches of government – executive, parliamentary and judicial – has been profound. Its influence is evident in legislative reform initiatives, child-focused budget initiatives and social protection measures, in human rights-based approaches to programming for women and children, and in the adoption of regional child rights charters.

In the private sphere, the Convention is helping encourage greater awareness of child rights in business, schools, families and communities, with the strong support of non-governmental organizations in particular. In the media, too, its effects are seen in the greater use of child rights language and a better understanding of critical issues, in the development of codes of conduct for reporting on children, and especially in the greater focus on child protection issues and violations. And although there is no systematic way to qualify this impact, there is ample evidence that it is taking place.

Legislative reform initiatives

Over the past two decades, around 70 States parties to the Convention have enacted consolidated children's statutes as part of law reform efforts to support child rights. Moreover, 12 States parties to the Convention have implemented these codes in response to an express recommendation by the Committee on the Rights of the Child. Most of these codes are based on frameworks for child protection that encompass a broad range of legal traditions, including civil law, common law, Islamic law and plural law.

In Latin America in particular, frameworks have been introduced that recognize the civil and political rights of children, as well as their economic, social and cultural rights – which tend to cover a substantial portion, if not all, of the Convention. In Eastern Europe, especially the countries of the former Soviet Union, the tendency is for child rights statutes that are more general in scope, citing an express or implied intention to undergo further reforms in the future.

A number of these States parties have one or more dimensions of human rights-based approaches in the design of their statutes. This implies that they have an explicit reference to international frameworks, present children as the subject of rights with the capacity to claim their rights, and identify duty bearers to implement child rights legislation. Other countries make an express reference to the Convention as a principal aim of their legislation.

Child–focused budget initiatives

Implementing the provisions of the Convention on the Rights of the Child has financial implications for States parties. Prioritizing children's rights in public expenditure requires political will and progressive financial commitment from the government. Budget analysis of how policy goals are being realized is an important step towards designing public financing mechanism that prioritized children's rights.

One example of this type of analysis is in South Africa, where child rights budgetary efforts have been led by the non-governmental organization Institute for Democracy in South Africa (IDASA). This independent organization monitors the public finances, and through its Children's Budget Project assesses whether government expenditure is helping the Government meet its obligations to children's rights and alleviate poverty.

Another example is provided by Ecuador, where a deep economic crisis in 1999 threatened social spending. UNICEF Ecuador partnered with the Government to analyse the impact of budgetary decisions on children, and make recommendations on social-sector allocations. The results have led to a regular framework for linking social and economic decision-making.

Human rights-based approach to cooperation

The human rights-based approach to programming is championed by UNICEF and others as a paradigm to ensure that children's rights are enacted in policy and practice. It has been highly influential in both industrialized and developing countries since its introduction in 1999. For more on this framework, see panel, pages 12–13.

Regional child rights charters

Regional bodies have also codified child rights into legislation. The African Charter on the Rights and Welfare of the Child was adopted in 1990. The European Union has a convention on the exercise of child rights, adopted by the Council of Europe in 1996. Although regional bodies such as the African Union and the European Union cannot ratify the Convention, the strong support they have shown for its provisions can be seen in their programmes and policies. For example, the EU is currently adopting a stronger framework of child rights based on the Convention to ensure that children are protected against abuses perpetrated through the Internet.

The private sector

The private sector has become an increasingly important stakeholder in international development through global partnerships for health, education and HIV and AIDS in particular. This growing participation has been recognized by the Committee on the Rights of the Child, which devoted its 2002 day of general discussion to the theme of 'The private sector as service provider and its role in implementing child rights'.

Like regional organizations, private sector entities cannot sign or ratify the Convention. But they are also demonstrating strong support for the treaty by their actions, whether as partners in building a protective environment or in direct supply of essential services. A noteworthy achievement is the Code of Conduct for the Protection of Children from Sexual Exploitation in Tourism. This resulted from collaboration between private tourism operators and the global End Child Prostitution, Child Pornography and Trafficking of Children for Sexual Purposes network. The Code commits the tourism industry to proactively seek ways of protecting children rights, and most of all to ensure that children are not exploited for commercial sexual purposes.

The media
By bringing attention to issues affecting children, the media have a unique role in realizing child rights. Greater awareness of child rights deprivations and violations is in part due to increased media focus on these issues. For example, the British Broadcasting Corporation, the world's largest public broadcaster, has a dedicated portal on children's rights and issues on its website.

As the global media industry has expanded, advocates for child rights have taken a strong lead in encouraging corporations to follow ethical standards in their reporting. UNICEF's Principles for Ethical Reporting on Children and other guidelines have promoted such codes to ensure that media reporting on children does not stereotype them as victims of abuse and poverty, per-

petrators of crimes or objects of charity. It is also critical that the best interests of children are respected in reporting on them. In Brazil, the Agency for Child Rights monitors how children are portrayed in the media, and issues league tables on negative portrayal. It also endows awards to create incentives for sensitive and ethical coverage.

Religious leaders
Religious leaders can have an important role in ensuring greater realization of children's rights. As respected and influential members of societies and communities, they can galvanize actions in favour of children's survival and development, protection and participation, and challenge practices, customs and norms that discriminate against or undermine theses rights. Throughout history, and across religions and cultures, compassion and care for children have been strong ethical, moral and spiritual values that denote a common understanding of the importance of protecting individuals at their youngest and most vulnerable age.

Across the world, religious leaders are working as advocates for child rights. One such example is found in Afghanistan, where since late 2001, UNICEF and its partners have worked closely with religious leaders to expand access to education for girls and foster improved child survival and health. Another example is provided by Ethiopia, where Muslim, Protestant and Orthodox leaders agreed to devote a 'religious week' to the issue of HIV and AIDS, using their extensive networks, influence and goodwill to address the stigma and discrimination associated with HIV.

Non-governmental organizations
Non-governmental organizations are among the primary agents engaged in actively promoting and realizing children's

rights. Their numerous efforts spurred and sustained the process that resulted in the drafting and finalization of the Convention in the late 1970s and the 1980s. The NGO Group for the Convention on the Rights of the Child, a network of 80 international and national organizations, was formed in 1983 to promote and actively participate in the drafting of the treaty.

Article 45 of the Convention provides a designated role for NGOs in monitoring its implementation by States parties. The NGO Group's liaison unit, supports the participation of non-governmental organizations, particularly national coalitions, in the reporting process to the Committee on the Rights of the Child. One important area of work that the unit facilitates is the compilation and submission of alternative reports on national implementation of the Convention to the Committee.

Advocates and individuals
The Convention has inspired individuals, both adults and children, to dedicate themselves tirelessly to promoting and defending children's rights. These advocates, who range from child activists to international celebrities, are instrumental in raising awareness of critical concerns and vulnerabilities and making direct representations to those in power to seek and effect change.

See References, pages 90–92.

for their care, protection and rehabilitation. Those who have lost parents, face extreme poverty or difficult family circumstances, or are differently abled may require access to alternative care. Policies and programmes that aim to support children and families, promote family reunification and establish appropriate use and conditions of alternative care are not always well developed at the national and district levels.

Building national child protection systems

Traditionally, the many dimensions of child protection have been championed by strong advocates – often non-governmental organizations – that work to prevent, reverse or ameliorate rights violations in a specific area. There are many organizations and individuals engaged in combating HIV and AIDS, for example; others are involved in preventing children from being recruited by armed forces or groups, and still others work to prevent violence against children and bring perpetrators to justice. These efforts, both individually and collectively, have done much to bring previously hidden issues to the fore and have spurred unprecedented changes in laws, budgets, research, programmes, advocacy and behaviours.

Issue-specific initiatives are steadily being complemented by a broader approach to child protection, which aims to create a protective environment for children across the entire breadth of society from birth to adulthood. The protective environment concept embodies the spirit of the Convention and other human rights treaties in envisaging a world where all the necessary elements are in place to protect children from all forms of violence, exploitation and unnecessary separation from their families. It provides a framework that embraces advances in legislation, policies, services, advocacy, practices and child participation to minimize vulnerability and strengthen children's protection from abuse. It presages a world in which every child grows up knowing there is a fabric of protective measures that work in a cohesive and integrated way to protect him or her from violence, exploitation and abuse, and provides justice and rehabilitation if abuses take place. Such an environment not only provides a bulwark against the web of risks and vulnerabilities that underlie many forms of abuse, it also improves the health, education and well-being of children, and boosts development progress.

A comprehensive child protection system facilitates the implementation of eight key interconnected actions that need to be pursued in the creation of a protective environment for children:

Commit governments to ensuring holistic protection for children. Adequate budgets for children's rights, comprehensive social welfare policies, ample recourse to justice, responsive social services and skilled personnel are required to set the foundation for a protective environment. Greater access to social protection services should be provided to marginalized and vulnerable families.

Pass and enforce laws that comprehensively address child protection concerns. This begins with ratification and implementation of international child rights standards and strengthening of national protection legislation. Having the appropriate laws in place is important, but legislation must also be consistently and accountably implemented, and impunity ended for crimes against children.

Provide correct information from credible sources on viable alternatives to existing attitudes, behaviours and practices that violate children's rights. This entails enabling communities to challenge the social norms and traditions that are injurious to children, and to support those that are protective. Community-based action should be complemented by public awareness campaigns addressing entrenched attitudes, beliefs and harmful practices that undermine child protection.

Promote open discussion of child protection issues. Silence is a major impediment to securing government com-

Building national child protection systems that seek to establish a protective environment for children reduces their vulnerability to violence, abuse and exploitation. *Indigenous and Afro-descendant children sit on a low wall in the rural eastern town of Yaviza in Darién Province, Panama.*

Child rights in Sierra Leone

Sierra Leone has experienced steady improvement in security and political stability since a decade of armed conflict ended in 2002. Peaceful national democratic elections were held in 2007, and efforts to strengthen government institutions and promote reconciliation are being pursued. Economic growth returned during the post-conflict period, averaging about 7.7 per cent per year between 2003 and 2007, driven mostly by the agriculture and mining sectors.

Sierra Leone ratified the Convention on the Rights of the Child in June 1990 and its two Optional Protocols in September 2001 (on the Sale of Children, Child Prostitution and Child Pornography) and May 2002 (on the Involvement of Children in Armed Conflict). These commitments were subsequently enshrined in national legislation through the 2007 Child Rights Act – which supersedes all other national laws and is considered compatible with the Convention and the African Charter on the Rights and Welfare of the Child.

Protecting children while restoring security

The Child Rights Act forms the basis of a stronger framework for protecting child rights. However, the road to its implementation is long. The country still lags in economic, social and human development. Although richly endowed with mineral resources, Sierra Leone ranked at the bottom of 177 countries and territories in the United Nations Development Programme's most recent *Human Development Index*. It has been strongly affected by the 2008-2009 global economic downturn, which has curtailed financial flows to the country from trade, investment, remittances and aid. Sierra Leone has also been listed by the Food and Agriculture Organization of the United Nations as one of the countries most vulnerable to food insecurity.

The country's maternal and under-five mortality rates are the highest in the world, and nearly 40 per cent of children under five suffer from moderate or severe stunting. Basic and maternal health facilities and services and environmental health infrastructure are in short supply. One third of infants do not receive routine immunization in the form of three doses of diphtheria, pertussis and tetanus toxoid vaccine. Nearly 60 per cent of women deliver without the assistance of a skilled health attendant. Almost half of Sierra Leoneans have no access to improved drinking-water facilities, and roughly 7 in every 10 citizens are without adequate sanitation facilities. More than 30 per cent of children of primary-school-age are not enrolled in school, and there are moderate transition rates from primary school to secondary and tertiary education. Barriers to girls' education include child marriage – 62 per cent of girls marry before age 18, and 27 per cent before age 15 – and high levels of adolescent pregnancy.

During the past two decades, Sierra Leone has faced obstacles in promoting and protecting the rights of its children. Conflict, poverty, gender inequities and discriminatory cultural practices combine to undermine child rights. Despite the return of democracy and greater political stability in Sierra Leone, girls and women are still exposed to sexual violence, along with harmful traditional practices such as female genital mutilation/cutting. More than 90 per cent of women aged 15–49 are estimated to have undergone FGM/C.

During the decade-long civil conflict, children were recruited by both government and rebel forces. The Special Court for Sierra Leone, set up to try those responsible for the most serious violations of human rights, convicted all nine defendants – including former president Charles Taylor – of recruiting children to fight as combatants. Three defendants have been convicted of forcing marriage on girls and women, marking the first time that a court has upheld such a charge.

Sierra Leone is making strides to increase children's participation. The Truth and Reconciliation Commission for Sierra Leone, established to create an impartial documentation of human rights violations, has involved children in the process and given special attention to the experiences of children affected by the civil strife. In the same spirit, in 2001 the Government of Sierra Leone formed the Children's Forum Network, a child-to-child advocacy organization committed to creating linkages and spreading knowledge on child rights and responsibilities. The Children's Forum Network is currently working in all of Sierra Leone's 13 districts.

Challenges ahead

To make meaningful advances on child survival and development, the Government of Sierra Leone, in partnership with other stakeholders, faces the challenge of scaling up such essential services as immunization, micronutrient supplementation, maternal, newborn and child health care, quality education and environmental health facilities, and developing a national child protection system. These advances require continued stability and peace, and an environment supportive of the rights of women and children. Establishing and maintaining political stability and security throughout the West and Central Africa region will therefore be critical to realizing the rights of children in Sierra Leone and its neighbours during the years ahead.

See References, pages 90–92.

mitment, supporting positive practices and ensuring the involvement of children and families. Open discussion is imperative if a coordinated, collective consensus is to be reached and harmful practices abandoned. Young people should be empowered to discuss their concerns and rights to protection in their communities and families. The media should not be impeded in its efforts to address child protection abuses, nor survivors or investigators intimidated.

Promote meaningful child participation and empowerment. Children need to be involved as actors in their own protection. They need to know about their protection rights and learn ways to avoid and respond to risks. This involves life skills education, peer-to-peer advocacy and participation in the formulation of solutions to child protection.

Strengthen the protective role of families and communities. Building the capacity of parents, families and communities, including teachers, health and social workers, and police, to understand and realize child rights is essential to protecting children. Governments can support these efforts by making social services widely available and promoting the elimination of all forms of violence, abuse and exploitation against women and children.

Improve monitoring and oversight through better data collection, analysis and use. Despite considerable improvements in monitoring and data collection, too little is known about the extent of protection violations in industrialized and developing countries. National data collection systems should routinely collect this information, disaggregated by sex, age, geographical location and other vulnerability factors. International monitoring requires greater investment, expanded indicators and greater consensus regarding definitions of protection failures such as child labour and child marriage. Research and analysis of child protection challenges and evaluation of protection initiatives also need to be strengthened.

Enable a protective environment for children in emergencies. The complex nature of emergencies demands an integrated approach to child protection that embraces provision of essential services, social welfare, and agencies entrusted with law enforcement and justice. Impunity for human rights violations against children must end, and countries must respect the national and international legislation and commitments to protecting children caught up in emergencies. In particular, countries facing armed conflict must monitor and report grave violations of child rights and end impunity for these violations.

These interconnected elements work to strengthen the protection of children and reduce their vulnerability. They represent a human rights-based approach aimed at reducing disparities in children's access to the information, advice and services that can protect them, whether those disparities are based on geographical or economic obstacles or emerge from any kind of discrimination. The strategies to be pursued in relation to all the areas in which children are exploited or abused should contribute to the building of this protective environment, which is realized through an interconnected and holistic system of legislation, policies, regulations and services aimed at presenting and responding to protection-related risks.

Child protection systems encompass services, procedures, policies and partnerships that protect children from violence, abuse and exploitation, and provide recourse to justice and rehabilitation when violations of these rights occur. Vital services include those that seek to tackle poverty, support and educate parents and other family members, prioritize physical safety, facilitate early detection and reporting of abuses, protect children's rights when they come into conflict with the law and contact with alternative care, and ensure that children's right to an identity is met.

Just as the concept of a protective environment includes the provision of key services, so children will be better protected from abuse and exploitation if they are benefiting from the health, education and other services to which they have a right. The flip side of this is that the protection of children becomes more difficult if they are not provided for as they should be. Children's rights to survival, development, protection and participation are fundamentally interrelated. Education is particularly vital, because it not only can provide a safe space and an essential point of contact with teachers who are able to assess children's mental and physical conditions on a daily basis, it also increases students' life skills and knowledge, making them better able to avoid risky situations and protect themselves. Every additional year spent in school increases the chances of children avoiding hazardous child labour or other forms of exploitation, which is why the nexus linking education and protection is such a potent promoter of child rights.

PARTICIPATION

Participation is one of the guiding principles of the Convention on the Rights of the Child, yet it is arguably taken less seriously than the other key principles of universality, the best interests of the child, and survival and development. To some extent, child participation may be seen as

Child Friendly Cities: An international initiative promoting child participation in local government

A 'child friendly city' is defined as any local system of governance, urban or rural, large or small, committed to fulfilling children's rights under the Convention. The international Child Friendly Cities Initiative (CFCI) was launched in 1996 to act on the resolution passed during the second United Nations Conference on Human Settlements (Habitat II) to make cities livable places for all. The conference declared that the well-being of children is the ultimate indicator of a healthy habitat, a democratic society and good governance.

The initiative reflects the growing urbanization of global societies, with half the world's population now living in cities, and the increasing importance of municipalities in political and economic decision-making that affects child rights. An international secretariat for Child Friendly Cities was created in 2000 at UNICEF Innocenti Research Centre in Florence, Italy. Consistent with the centre's mission, the secretariat collects, documents, distils and disseminates experience on local frameworks to implement the Convention on the Rights of the Child and achieve the Millennium Development Goals.

A child-friendly city aims to guarantee children's rights to essential services, such as health, education, shelter, safe water and decent sanitation, and protection from violence, abuse and exploitation. It also seeks to empower young citizens to influence decisions about their city, express their opinion on the city they want, and participate in family community and social life. It promotes children's rights to walk safely in the streets by themselves, meet friends and play, live in an unpolluted environment with green spaces, participate in cultural and social events and be an equal citizen of

their city with access to every service, without discrimination of any kind.

The process of establishing child-friendly cities involves the following nine elements that promote child rights: participation in decision making; a child-friendly legal framework; a city-wide child rights strategy; a child rights unit or coordinating mechanisms; child impact assessment and evaluation; a children's budget; a regular State of the City's Children report; advocating child rights; and independent advocacy for children.

During the past decade, a number of cities and municipalities across the world have made the political decision to become 'child-friendly'. Child-friendly cities programmes have been adopted by many European cities to sensitize mayors and city councils on child rights, ensure that children feature in the local political agenda and promote city-level policies for children. London, for instance, published its third *State of London's Children Report* in 2007. In Italy, the Ministry of the Environment coordinates the child-friendly cities initiatives, which have been adopted by many towns and cities. Child councils are a favoured model of child participation in Italy and other European countries, providing a formal mechanism for children's views to be expressed within local administrations. These councils are often instigators of child-friendly initiatives, promoting participatory policy-making and greater mobility and civil engagement of children and young people.

The developing world also has an important number of initiatives. In the Philippines, child-friendly cities programmes started in the late 1990s. The

initiative has a national dimension through a goal-oriented framework that aims to promote child-rights principles at every level, from the family through community to the city or region. Since 1998, the national government has been giving 'Presidential awards' for child-friendly cities and municipalities. In South Africa, the Greater Johannesburg Metropolitan Council's initiative includes the development of a Metropolitan Programme of Action for Children. The programme empowers children to directly influence local laws, incorporates child rights into city planning and allocates major resources to the city's most deprived children.

In the Ecuadorian cities of Cuenca, Guayaquil, Quito, Riobamba and Tena, children help define criteria for a child-friendly city. Under the auspices of La Ciudad que Queremos (The City We Want) initiative, children and adolescents participate in municipal decisions and promote their own rights. In Georgia, the Children and Youth Parliament of Georgia has become a primary forum for children and young people to express their views, gain skills in governance and raise awareness on child rights.

Despite its 13-year history, the Child Friendly Cities Initiative is still nascent, and many of the initiatives that are under way have yet to be comprehensively monitored and evaluated. Yet it remains a strong step towards fuller and more meaningful child participation in community decisions that affect them. Building on the progress achieved by the initiative will be critical to fulfiling child rights in a world that is becoming ever more urbanized.

See References, pages 90–92.

more controversial, challenging or difficult to implement than measures supporting child survival, development and protection because it is based on presenting children as rights holders rather than as recipients of charity. Also, there is less experience in this area among the child rights community than in survival, development and protection.

The Convention does not use the term 'participation' or explicitly state that children have a right to participate – except as a goal for children with disabilities (article 23). But it requires that their views be heard in relation to all matters that affect them and that their views be given due weight in accordance with their age and maturity (article 12). This right is part of a broader body of participation rights that children hold, starting with the right to freedom of expression (article 13), thought, conscience and religion (14), association (15), the right to privacy (16) and access to appropriate information (17) that provides the basis for the child's right to participate. The Convention refers to children's "evolving capacity" for decision-making – a revolutionary concept in international law[13] – and this has profoundly influenced the practice of organizations working in the field during the past 20 years.

The right of children to participate is a fundamental component of respecting them as holders of their own rights. Being able to influence decisions that affect an individual is one of the defining characteristics of human rights principles. When it comes to designing opportunities for children to participate, conditions need to be adjusted in accordance with a child's age and maturity. They should not be pressured, constrained or influenced in ways that might prevent them from freely expressing their opinions or leave them feeling manipulated. Effective and meaningful participation depends on many factors, including the child's developing capabilities, the openness of parents and other adults to dialogue, and safe spaces

© UNICEF/NYHQ2009-0249/Josh Estey

Children should be empowered to participate in the decisions and actions that affect them, according to their age and maturity. *A 13-year-old seventh-grade student and her classmates make posters during a life-skills training session in Kim Dong Lower Secondary School in Lao Cai Province, Viet Nam. The school provides life-skills training on child rights, health, HIV and AIDS and other issues.*

within the family, community and society that allow such dialogue. It also depends on stakeholders being willing to take children's views into consideration. Much of the practice of child participation is based on children's right to expression in all matters affecting them – this has, to an increasing extent, guided legal processes in decisions relating to custody following divorce or disputes between parents and authorities over children taken into care.

The vast majority of public decisions affecting children are made, however, without considering the views of or involving children. Policies have traditionally focused on welfare, perceiving children as passive recipients of care and services, not public actors. In general, children are rarely able to exercise any influence over the resources allocated in their name. Much of the work of government and civil society is carried out without explicit recognition of children and young people. Interventions are implemented on behalf of children rather than with them.

Children are not generally seen as social and political actors. In most countries, individuals do not vote in national and local elections until they reach age 18. Children, therefore, often have no formal place at the decision-making table, and adult-controlled mechanisms are likely to be required for chil-

PARTICIPATION RIGHTS

According to the Convention on the Rights of the Child, every child has the right to participation through:

	ARTICLES
Respect for the views of the child	12
Freedom of expression	13
Freedom of thought, conscience and religion	14
Freedom of association	15
Right to privacy	16
Access to information: mass media	17

Source: Derived from the Convention on the Rights of the Child.

Child rights in India

India, home to one fifth of the world's children, ratified the Convention on the Rights of the Child in December 1992. Since then, rapid economic growth, averaging 4.5 per cent annually between 1990 and 2007, has lifted millions out of poverty and combined with government action to improve trends in child survival and development. According to national sources, the national under-five mortality rate fell sharply from 117 per 1,000 live births in 1990 to 72 in 2007. Use of improved drinking water sources rose from 62 per cent in 1992–1993 to 88 per cent in 2005–2006. Primary school attendance rates for girls 6–10 years old climbed from 61 to 81 per cent over the same period, helping lift the gender parity rate for primary education from 0.82 to 0.96.

Deprivations and disparities remain large, despite economic progress

Despite this marked progress, many challenges for realizing child rights in India remain. Partly because of its immensity, India experiences child rights deprivations in greater absolute numbers than any other country. Each year, 1 million newborns die during the first month of life; another million die between 29 days and five years. Almost 55 million children under five are underweight for their age. In excess of 20 million children of primary school age are not attending school. More than 40 per cent of the population currently lives on less than $1.25 per day, 128 million people have no access to improved drinking-water sources, and a staggering 665 million defecate in the open.

Rising incomes have been accompanied by widening disparities in income, education, access to health care and development outcomes. The 2005–2006 National Family Health Survey shows sharp divergences in access to essential services and key development outcomes across caste, ethnic, gender and wealth strata. These disparities extend to child protection, given the country's moderate rate of birth registration (69 per cent) and high rate of child marriage. Despite legislation prohibiting child marriage, the latest household surveys indicate that an estimated 47 per cent of women aged 20–24, and 16 per cent of men aged 20–49, were married or in union before age 18. In addition, the country's skewed sex ratio at birth and high level of child labour remain significant challenges.

Concerted efforts are yielding results

The Government of India, its partners and a multitude of non-governmental organizations have made determined efforts to reduce child deaths, expand access to health care and get children into primary school. The country is also making headway towards identifying child protection violations and creating legal means of redress. It is beginning to address material disparities by targeting essential services towards marginalized groups such as scheduled castes, scheduled tribes (the indigenous peoples, or Adivasis) and others who suffer entrenched discrimination. A National Commission for the Protection of Child Rights was established by the Government in March 2007 to monitor proper enforcement of child rights. In addition, a comprehensive plan called the Integrated Child Protection Scheme has been set up to protect vulnerable children.

Women-led and women-focused organizations are thriving in India, which is home to some of the world's most innovative institutions empowering women in the community, the workplace and government. Similarly, non-governmental organizations and voluntary groups have for decades been among India's most energetic advocates for child rights. An example is Balkan-Ji-Bari. Founded in 1923, this organization has become a recreational and educational institution for impoverished Adivasi children, providing vocational training, vaccinations and other services.

Young people are showing the way to overcoming some of the key obstacles to fulfilling child rights. In 1990, child labourers involved with the Concerned for Working Children organization launched their own association – Bhima Sangha, which has become an international model for children's participation. Beginning in 1997, Bhima Sangha has established *makkala panchayats,* or children's councils, that run parallel to adult councils. In the state of Kerala, the government has institutionalized child participation through Bala Sabhas or children's neighbourhood groups. There are 45,417 clubs in the state, with around 800,000 participants.

Challenges ahead

Widespread and entrenched exploitation, gender discrimination, caste bias and other social problems in India will not be overcome overnight, and it is uncertain how the 2008–2009 global fuel, food and economic crises will affect the country's social progress. As all three threaten to undermine India's economic growth, there is a grave risk that the share of people living in absolute poverty will increase, possibly slowing or even stalling recent moderate gains in child survival, health and education.

The Government of India and other stakeholders are working towards fulfilling child rights – and young people themselves are voicing their priorities and embracing community involvement. Their continued participation and leadership will be critical to achieving continued human progress in India during the years to come.

See References, pages 90–92.

dren's opinions to be represented. Children involved in political processes are often considered as technical actors who can provide useful information, rather than as citizens or political actors with rights to uphold and interests to defend.

At conferences, adults may listen to children, but when it comes to the important decisions, children are often excluded. Youth parliaments may be little more than debating clubs where children learn about governance and politics. Some attempts at involving young people, moreover, are tokenistic – done more for the image of the adult organization bringing them together than for the benefit of the children themselves.

Children's participation has a vital role in empowering them in their own development. Through participation, girls and boys can learn vital life-skills and knowledge and take action to prevent and address abuse and exploitation. Participation initiatives are strengthened when children know and understand their rights. Consulting with children is critical to ensure that child survival, development and protection measures are adequate and appropriate.

There have been a growing number of initiatives in child participation since the Convention came into force in 1990. One highlight was the 2002 UN General Assembly Special Session on Children, an event that actively encouraged the participation of children in the principal decision-making body of the United Nations. More than 400 children from over 150 countries took part in the three-day Children's Forum that culminated in a common statement from the participants reflecting their views.

The 2006 UN Secretary-General's Study on Violence against Children was the first United Nations study to consult with children and reflect and incorporate their views and recommendations. Children and adolescents participated in national, regional and international consultations, together with policymakers. To disseminate the findings of the study, child-friendly versions were created for a range of age groups. Children and adolescents were also strongly represented at the November 2008 Third World Congress against the Sexual Exploitation of Children and Adolescents in Rio de Janeiro (Brazil).

It is increasingly being recognized that consulting children and adolescents is a practical way to ensure that policies and practices affecting them are effective. It is by no means easy to build permanent mechanisms whereby children and young people can influence public planning and budget decisions. But when this has been achieved, the results have been encouraging – not just in terms of the developmental benefits to the participating young people but also in terms of the

effectiveness of the community action that has emerged from their decisions.

One of the pioneering examples of child participation in governance has been the Brazilian city of Barra Mansa, which since 1998 has had a participatory budget council comprising 18 girls and 18 boys. These elected children monitor the wider municipal council's performance in addressing the needs of young people and are responsible for spending a portion of the budget.[14] Among other examples of children's participatory budgets are those of the populous Brazilian cities of Sao Paulo and Porto Alegre,[15] and Newcastle-upon-Tyne in the United Kingdom.[16]

These examples illustrate some of the benefits of meaningful children's participation, which has been shown to enhance democracy and inclusive governance and increase the relevance and effectiveness of development projects. Participation can also offer poor and marginalized children the chance to gain skills and experience that afford them opportunities for development, as well as provide knowledge of public services and a taste for citizenship.

In addition, child rights advocates are coming to recognize that participation by children and adolescents can play a vital part in protecting them from abuse, violence and exploitation.[17] Participation fosters the resilience of children and adolescents and can enable them to become agents of change and to resist the processes that result in their abuse. It can also help them recover if they are abused, not least through sharing their experiences with their peers.[18]

The theory and practice of children's participation is still in its infancy. But it has advanced significantly during the two decades since the Convention was adopted by the Member States of the United Nations. Moreover, the Convention has been a guiding force in encouraging greater child participation. Policymakers are becoming increasingly appreciative that involving young people in decision-making not only enhances children's development, protection and understanding of democracy, it improves outcomes for all. More children and young people are developing their capacity to participate and collaborate through youth organizations and networks to advocate for their rights.

A major development in this area has been the recent adoption of General Comment No. 12 on the right of a child to be heard by the Committee on the Rights of the Child. This marks the first time that the Committee has issued a General Comment on one of the treaty's guiding principles. The

Realizing child rights is pivotal to creating the world envisioned by the Millennium Declaration – one of peace, equity, tolerance, security, freedom, solidarity, respect for the environment and shared responsibility. *"I have a right to peace,"* read the slates of these children standing at the front of their classroom in Kabiline I Primary School in the village of Kabiline, Senegal.

General Comment provides guidance to Member States and other stakeholders to enhance their understanding and interpretation of the article; elaborates the scope of the legislation, policy and practice needed to achieve its full implementation; highlights positive approaches in its implementation; and proposes basic requirements for appropriate ways to give due weight to children's views in all matters that affect them.

Towards greater understanding and implementation of the Convention

The Convention on the Rights of the Child is not a only historic document, it is a moral compass that continues to guide people all over the world, in every culture and every region, as they strive to deal more sensitively and justly with children – from parents, teachers, doctors or police officers to government ministers charged with the responsibility of children's welfare and protection. It has already altered the landscape of children's rights. But its vision of a world in which those rights are universally valued and guaranteed is still far from being realized.

The remainder of this report looks at the challenges ahead, beginning with a selection of guest essays written by representatives of the main stakeholder groups that support the Convention: family and community; civil society and the media; development professionals; governments and international agencies; the private sector; and children, adolescents and youth.

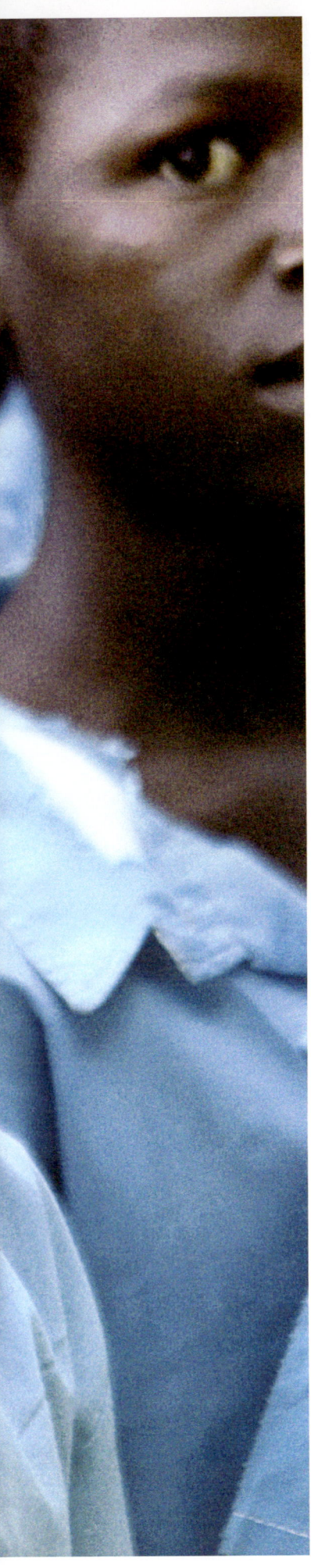

Perspectives on the Convention

The Convention on the Rights of the Child sets the standards for the care, treatment and protection of all children. Interpreting these standards and applying the measures required to realize the rights they safeguard relies on the actions of stakeholders, including parents, families and communities, civil society and the media, governments and international agencies, the private sector, advocates and activists, individuals and institutions, and children, adolescents and young people.

The perspectives of these stakeholders on the meaning and value of the Convention forms the basis of their actions to apply its provisions in their countries, communities, societies, households and organizations. Although proponents of the Convention on the Rights of the Child have a common goal – realizing the rights of all children, everywhere, at all times – the diverse nature of their experience, expertise and environments provide a rich vein of ideas and innovations in advocacy, policy and practice.

To mark the 20th anniversary of the Convention, *The State of the World's Children* has invited contributors from a variety of stakeholder groups to give their perspective, in 1,000 words or less, on what the Convention means to them and what they consider to be some of the critical issues it faces in the 21st century. The essays presented here are a selection of those received at the time of going to press in mid-2009; the full series is available on the UNICEF website at www. unicef.org/rightsite.

My identity, my rights: From child labourer to child rights activist

by Om Prakash Gurjar

Om Prakash Gurjar was born in Dwaarapur village of Alwar district, Rajasthan, to a family of bonded labourers. For many years, he was forced to work on the farm of the landlord as a bonded labourer. After being liberated with the help of Bachpan Bachao Andolan in 2002, he was educated and trained at Bal Ashram. Om Prakash has helped liberate many of the children of his village from child servitude and helped them enrol in school. He has emerged as an unparalleled warrior for child rights and was awarded the International Children's Peace Prize in 2006. At present, he is a young Bachpan Bachao Andolan activist and a student in the 11th grade.

In the village in India where I was born and raised, the notion of child rights does not exist. Our parents rear us through their hard work with duty and determination. If a family is able to save money, their children may be able to attend school. More often, however, the children have no option but to join their parents in farming and caring for cattle.

When boys are born, grandmothers stand at the threshold of the home and joyously beat a *thali*, metal plate, to announce the birth of a male child. In contrast, whenever a girl is born, the women of the family break an earthen pitcher at the entrance of the house. This act is also performed when there is a death in the family, and signifies to neighbours and village folk sadness that the child has been born a girl. The difference between a boy and a girl, and their respective value in home and by society, is clearly marked from the beginning.

I am the son of a father who once borrowed money from his landlord, who in return obliged him and my family to serve as bonded labourers. When I was five years old, before I could understand why I was compelled to work as a labourer, I was toiling on the landlord's farm. I worked with animals and crops, and wondered why I did not go to school like other children. Three years later, a group of activists of Bachpan Bachao Andolan, (Save the Childhood Movement) were travelling from village to village. Through outreach efforts to raise awareness about education and their campaigning against child servitude, they met me and other child labourers. Hearing them speak was the first time I realized that my childhood was being wasted, and that there were people who cared about saving it.

After getting to know our situation, the activists diligently worked to free us from bonded labour and child servitude. It was a difficult task, as neither our landlords nor our parents were prepared to consider that children had rights, or that there was anything wrong with child labour. At first, my parents shunned any kind of dispute. After much effort, however, the activists of Bachpan Bachao Andolan persuaded them to press for my release from servitude, and they also exerted pressure on the landlord to free me from service. Because of their dedication, I was eventually liberated.

After leaving bonded servitude, I went to Bal Ashram, a child rehabilitation home in Rajasthan, devoted to educating and training liberated bonded labourers. From the moment I arrived at Bal Ashram, I understood what child rights are. For the first time I observed and realized that here was a place where children's voices are heard, their opinions considered, and decisions made after taking their opinion into account. There was a panchayat (assembly) of child members who represented the students' interests and concerns in meetings with the managers and instructors. Gradually, through our teachers and the other children at Bal Ashram, I came to understand there are laws to promote and protect children like us. I learned that these laws not only apply in India but also

In India, to even have a chance of realizing child rights you must first be recognized by the law. This means that a child's own identity is the most significant factor in the cause of child rights.

throughout the world. Through these laws the rights of children have been articulated, and it is the collective responsibility of all to implement the standards that the Convention on the Rights of the Child and other child rights instruments set forth.

During my education and training at Bal Ashram, I took the initiative to talk about child rights in my school and surroundings. After being freed from bonded labour I was eager for education and also to help spread awareness about the challenges facing children like me. The local public school where I studied charged a fee of 100 rupees. I had read that public schools are supposed to be free. I raised this issue to a local magistrate and demanded adequate action. A petition was put to the Jaipur Court, the high bench of the state of Rajasthan where I live. The court decided that the school was obliged to return the money to the parents. My case was cited by the Rajasthan State Human Rights Commission, and now in the state of Rajasthan schools are prohibited from taking money from parents. Recently, when I was involved in the action of liberating bonded child labourers from *zari*, or gold thread, factories together with the activists of Bachpan Bachao Andolan, I observed how callous the conduct of government officials was with the liberated children. When I asked them to follow the rules in the Convention, they appeared ignorant that such rules exist.

In India, to even have a chance of realizing child rights you must first be recognized by the law. This means that a child's own identity is the most significant factor in the cause of child rights. Knowing this, I encouraged children from Dausa and Alwar Districts to claim their rights, and during birth registration campaigns, I assisted more than 500 children to formally register with the Government. Having a birth registration gives children rights both now and in the future.

Twenty years after the adoption of the Convention on the Rights of the Child, there is still little awareness of child rights in India, either among common people and even in many government organizations working for child rights. Although the Government of India has taken an initiative to safeguard child rights by setting up the Child Rights Protection Commission, its impact is yet to be fully felt. I believe that through the efforts of activists working for child rights all over the world, pressure must be exerted on the governments of the signatory nations of the Convention on the Rights of the Child to meet their obligations to children. Awareness must be raised on this issue, and countries must be made accountable for active implementation of child rights.

© UNICEF/BANA07-00011/Shehzad Noorami

An 8-year-old girl carries freshly moulded brick near Joydehpur on the outskirts of Dhaka, Bangladesh.

Sustainable fiscal policy: Investing in Chile's youth

by Andrés Velasco

Andrés Velasco was appointed as Chile's Minister of Finance in 2006. He received a bachelor's degree in economics from Yale University and a PhD in economics from Columbia University. Dr. Velasco has held a number of academic appointments and post-doctoral fellowships and is a leading expert in development economics. He has served in several positions in the Government of Chile, in addition to working as a consultant for the World Bank, the Inter-American Development Bank, the International Monetary Fund and several Central American governments. Dr. Velasco does not hold a political affiliation.

In 1990, the first Government of the Coalition of Parties for the Democracy – Concertación – assumed the call raised by the Convention on the Rights of the Child. Each Chilean Government since has taken action to fulfil this commitment. Important progress has been made in the area of child rights, particularly during the administration of President Bachelet, with the introduction of several new social programmes that focus on children's development and that are supported by a sustainable fiscal policy and a long-term vision.

Investment in Chile's children is socially and economically justified, and the sooner it begins, the bigger its impact can be. Numerous studies have gathered evidence on the positive long-term effects of preschool education, confirming that the first years of childhood are critical to the development of skills that accompany us throughout our lives. These studies demonstrate that children who receive quality preschool education will later have a better educational performance, a greater probability of enrolling in tertiary education, a higher future income and lower levels of criminal behaviour.

Childhood policies, particularly those intended to increase preschool attendance, positively affect fairness and equality of opportunity by offsetting the differences in children's backgrounds. Additionally, these policies are a powerful short-term tool to stimulate the female labour force participation rate in Chile, which, despite its recent improvements, remains below that of developed countries. Over 30 per cent of heads of households in the poorest sectors of the country are women, who have a higher need for free childcare provision. The public preschool provision and free childcare services favour not only these mothers by facilitating their entry in the labour market, but also their children, who benefit from greater family income, therefore becoming more likely to leave poverty behind.

In the first months of 2006, President Bachelet convened a Presidential Advisory Council made up of specialists of varied disciplines, with the mission of developing proposals for the reform of childhood policies in Chile. Most of these proposals, which set up a system based on rights protection to increase equality of opportunity, were implemented and funded by the Government in the following years.

In the context of this reform, the Integrated Child Protection System – Chile Crece Contigo – was created in 2007. This system includes a set of cross-sectoral actions that integrate children in a supportive network and monitor their growth and development. An important programme within Chile Crece Contigo is the 'Biopsychosocial' Development Programme, which benefits children from the womb to four years of age by combining health screenings with initiatives geared to stimulate them and avoid lags in their development. The coverage of this programme has gradually expanded to reach a larger age range and geographical spread of children, resulting in the participation of more than 1 million children in the programme this year alone. Additionally, by adopting

Investment in Chile's children is socially and economically justified, and the sooner it begins, the bigger its impact can be.

a child rights-based approach to social policy, the Government established an automatic subsidy per child for lower-income families, which benefits nearly 1.4 million people. Currently, Congress is reviewing a draft law that institutionalizes Chile Crece Contigo and assures its future financing.

Taking into account the importance of preschool education for the development of children and the insertion of their mothers in the labour market, the Government committed to a historical plan to increase preschool coverage. In the four years of this administration, public supply of free childcare centres will have increased fivefold at a rate of 900 new rooms per year, offering places this year for a total of 85,000 children from 0–2 years old from the poorest 40 per cent of the population. This represents an increase in coverage from 3 per cent to 17 per cent.

During the present administration, pre-kindergarten education was integrated into the Government's school voucher system, thereby guaranteeing it for all children. Today, these vouchers benefit approximately 120,000 children and help provide them with schooling and meal programmes. Resources were also invested to extend the school day of pre-kindergarten and kindergarten students for the subsidized schools that request it.

Finally, the differentiated voucher scheme for the most vulnerable children enrolled in primary education was implemented in 2008. This voucher not only increased resources for the most disadvantaged students, it also introduced incentives to increase the quality of education students received. This scheme reaffirms the principle of non-discrimination, ensuring that equality of opportunity for students regardless of their socio-economic status becomes a reality. The differentiated voucher will benefit 750,000 students per year.

None of these measures would have been possible without the combination of two fundamental factors: the will of the President to give child protection policies the priority they deserve, and a serious macroeconomic policy that assures the resources needed for its implementation – regardless of the external shocks that are affecting the economy. An important benefit of the fiscal surplus rule applied in Chile is that expenditure is not linked to the transitory components of income, which, in the context of the current crisis, allows for the use of the resources saved by our country during the boom years. This has enabled us to ensure the continuity of the social protection system that is the seal of the Government of President Bachelet and that is at the heart of the Convention on the Rights of the Child.

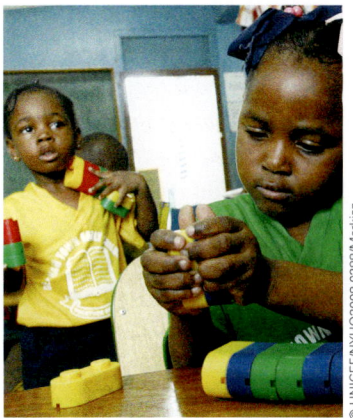

© UNICEF/NYHQ2008-0288/Markisz

A girl plays with colourful plastic blocks at Denham Town Basic School in the parish of Kingston and St. Andrew, Jamaica.

Life on the streets: Millions of children remain homeless, without care and protection

by Hanna Polak

*Academy Award-nominated film-maker **Hanna Polak** graduated from the Cinematography Institute of the Russian Federation. In connection with her moviemaking, she has been involved in charitable activities in Russia and founded, and later collaborated with, Active Child Aid to help underprivileged children all over the world.*

The fight for the rights of children, for their protection and well-being, is of the utmost necessity. Whenever this fight is lost – as it is when a homeless child dies on the street – we must question how much is being done, by nations, legislators, communities and individuals, to protect children from the saddest fate of all.

For those working with abused or homeless children, and for these children themselves, the vision of the Convention on the Rights of the Child can seem light years away. 'Street' children are usually deprived of almost all the rights embodied in the Convention. Having escaped homes and orphanages fraught with violence and neglect, they continue to experience a cruel reality. Many are forced into child labour, and nearly all become victims of sexual exploitation.

These children often experience violent abuse from the very people and authorities entrusted with their care and protection. They suffer from various medical afflictions, many of which require hospitalization. To curb their hunger and loneliness, they sniff 'glue' and soon become addicted to hard drugs. All they see is brutality and exploitation. Short-term relationships – with homeless children and pets – are used as a substitute for long-term, caring, sustained relationships. In this harsh environment, where every day is a fight for survival, homeless children invariably commit crimes and often end up in prison. Death regularly crosses their path; they see the passing of homeless friends or are brutally murdered themselves, they die of drug overdoses or disease.

Homeless children live in inhumane conditions. They sleep in stairways, garbage containers and underground tunnels. In the winter they take comfort from hot water pipes, whose steam provides them with much needed warmth. They scour for food in garbage bins and dumps. They are forced to live an adult life on the margins of society while they are still children. Yet, despite the uncertainties of their lives, they sing, they dance and they dream.

The appalling situations these children experience demand an urgent response. It is our duty to ensure their rights under the Convention are realized, to get them off the streets and out of the garbage dumps. This does not mean that nothing has been done – but rather that not enough is being done, at all levels. Governments must honour their obligations and do much more to assist abused, abandoned, and homeless children. Communities should play a part in caring for their children. Individual actions can also be powerful catalysts of social change.

We can raise awareness of the problem of child poverty and homelessness. We can influence public opinion by delivering messages to politicians and authorities who have the resources and the opportunities to improve the situation. We can attract the attention of the media, which has tremendous power to influence public opinion and spark change for the better. Through minor efforts, we can be major advocates for change.

An example of this can be seen in Moscow, where in recent years members of the media have begun to examine the problem of homeless youth. Their efforts prompted the then president

Even the smallest effort can bring about the greatest victory – saving the life of one of these beautiful children. They want nothing more than to have the childhood countries acknowledge in the Convention on the Rights of the Child.

and current prime minister, Vladimir Putin, to address the issue of child homelessness. He enacted policies that resulted in the building of new orphanages in the Moscow region and the expansion of programmes to prevent children from living on the streets.

Even when the majority of people and politicians in a society agree on the necessity of a code of rights for children, and that everyone has equal value and should be treated with respect, implementation of human rights for children remains far from universal. Disparities in income, living conditions, access to essential services, and struggles between different societal groups often result in many children missing out on having their basic rights to survival and development, protection and participation. This is why raising awareness on the fundamental imperative of fulfilling child rights must be an ongoing process.

12- and 15-year-old girls talk and read in their bedroom at the 'Sparrows' shelter for children living and working on the streets in Tbilisi, Georgia.

I believe all government leaders have a responsibility to implement essential and abiding human rights, backed by legislation appropriate for their respective countries. A sign of an evolved society is when its vulnerable groups – including children, the elderly, and those living with disability – are treated with respect. The transition countries of Central and Eastern Europe and the Commonwealth of Independent States are experiencing special challenges with regard to the issue of human rights for the vulnerable, owing to the fact that some population groups in these nations have been suppressed and denied equal opportunities. Furthermore, the non-government sector is still nascent, as the solutions to prevalent social problems previously lay exclusively in the hands of state-run agencies and organizations. This will only change with time, as individuals and non-governmental organizations become more active in their respective societies.

The Children of Leningradsky, a documentary film I made in 2005, is an intimate portrait of homeless children in Russia. The project originated from a desire to examine the situation of the neglected child from many different angles. The documentary depicts the tragic fate of children who have been left behind, who have not been protected and who are being denied their rights. At the time the movie was made, Russian authorities estimated there were approximately 30,000 homeless children living on the streets and in the railway stations of Moscow.

This documentary was a cry for help for these children, and it has been heard. Internationally, and in Russia, media coverage and screenings, university lectures, panel discussions and other well-attended events have raised awareness about homeless youth. My film and others like it offer tangible contributions to the discussion of child rights, while also making people aware of the ongoing tragedy of homeless and neglected children the world over.

Even the smallest effort can bring about the greatest victory – saving the life of one of these beautiful children. They want nothing more than to actually *be* children, with all of the fun, freedom and security that childhood should entail – and that countries acknowledge in the Convention on the Rights of the Child.

Express yourself: Promoting freedom of expression for children through education

by Marjorie Scardino

Marjorie Scardino is Chief Executive of Pearson, the international education and media business made up of Pearson Education, Penguin and the Financial Times Group. Until January 1997, she was chief executive of The Economist Group, and, prior to 1985, she was a partner in a law firm in Savannah, Georgia (United States). Marjorie and her husband, Albert Scardino, founded and published the Pulitzer Prize-winning newspaper The Georgia Gazette. *They have three children.*

Around the world, we yearn for economic and political self-determination, because we yearn for the liberty to express ourselves. Our expressions – whether words or pictures, art or music, the physical sport of soccer or the intellectual sport of numbers – hold our ideas, our dreams and the images we have of ourselves. A child without education and freedom of expression cannot develop. That has been the goal of the Convention on the Rights of the Child, and it is a goal that should move us all, and has for two decades.

My perspective is from the private sector, as head of an education and media company that tries to help people of all ages in more than 60 countries express themselves by helping to educate them both formally and informally. "It is the education which gives a man a clear conscious view of his own opinions and judgments, a truth in developing them, an eloquence in expressing them, and a force in urging them," religious and educational philosopher John Henry Newman wrote back in 1852. Twenty years ago, the Convention outlined a similar principle: that if a child had a 'right' to education, then he might as a consequence obtain access to the information and freedom of expression that would, in the words of the Preamble, help him be "fully prepared to live an individual life in society."

While the Convention includes more than 50 articles, I want to focus here only on the power of those three areas – education, information and expression. These have enlightened specific initiatives in our company and shown us how to play a role – often in partnership with governments and non-governmental organizations – in ensuring that children have access to education and that they have diverse experiences in the process.

To take three examples that we know well:

In Angola, we are working with the Ministry of Education and the Monteno Institute for Language and Literacy, a South African not-for-profit group, to introduce 1 million students to textbooks in the indigenous languages they speak at home but have never seen in print. This is an undertaking that Angola's Government believes will raise its struggling literacy rate.

With partners such as the Government of the United Kingdom and not-for-profit organizations JumpStart, BookTrust and Book Aid International, we have engaged in large-scale projects that get books into the hands of children and encourage parents to read aloud to them.

One of our websites, 'Poptropica', combines gaming with education – in a way that has attracted 40 million children in 70 countries speaking 90 different languages – to engage with each other in learning math, science, history and other subjects.

Too often, we assume that a private company's purpose is profits, and its concentration on the larger society is just an obligatory sidelight. A private company dedicated to the long term is surely sustained by profits, because it has no other livelihood; but this company is

As the Convention on the Rights of the Child celebrates its 20th anniversary, the private sector has every reason to be grateful for the emphasis the treaty brings regarding the power of developing a new generation of citizens.

driven and defined by the social purposes it serves. Helping children expand their mind and find their voices through education and information is a large part of our purpose.

There are, of course, challenges facing all organizations, private and public, trying to help achieve the freedom of expression goals of the Convention. Commercial broadcasters and newspapers, as all media, have been pressured and changed by the economics of the digital age. The effect could be to reduce both the outlets and the programming that might speak to children. Education budgets in many countries are underfunded in this time of economic strain. In some countries, stimulus funding will help ease the pressure, but cuts will still be made. Around the world, countries face a teacher shortage that could jeopardize their bold commitment to educational improvement, imperilling the UN's Millennium Development Goal 2 to have primary education available to all children by 2015.

Students queue for class at Timnin El-Tahta, a public school in the north-east Beqaa Valley region, Lebanon.

We will have to be bold if we are to overcome the consequences of these issues. But, still, there are plenty of reasons to be hopeful that the next 20 years can become a time for information, learning and human expression. Perhaps the greatest reason to be hopeful is that the digital revolution simply enables us to share stories and ideas in inclusive ways that were never possible before. Technology allows a wealth of dazzling and instructive content to be distributed to children all over the world on mobile phones and computers – allowing them to learn at their own pace and in their own space and time. In some countries, wireless technology has leapfrogged landlines, winging educational material to remote areas previously out of bounds economically and physically.

Allowing children to organize themselves into social networks also helps them find their voices. Getting together virtually and hearing each other speak helps children of all nationalities and backgrounds to forge – or at least identify – common bonds that were once either invisible or out of reach. Although these networks may need some rules, they can be powerful tools of social exchange, accentuating what connects us, rather than what divides us.

Of course, even the very latest, most beautiful software cannot replace teachers – those flesh-and-blood emissaries of facts, figures, understanding, stimulation, excitement and just pure magic for millions of children every year. But the software can help multiply them by automating some of the teacher's functions: collecting diagnostic information about the child's learning pace and chronic needs; allowing children to assess themselves and plug gaps in their learning; delivering information to schools and parents that help them fulfil their role.

As the Convention on the Rights of the Child celebrates its 20th anniversary, the private sector has every reason to be grateful for the emphasis it brings to the power of developing a new generation of citizens, and the reminder that children are the flowers of our societies. We take great joy in having been provoked by the Convention's ideas, and in looking forward to what we can do to promote them in the future.

Ishmael Beah, born in 1980 in Sierra Leone, is the author of best-selling A Long Way Gone: Memoirs of a boy soldier. He is UNICEF's Advocate for Children Affected by War, a member of the Human Rights Watch Children's Advisory Committee, co-founder of the Network for Young People Affected by War (NYPAW) and president of the Ishmael Beah Foundation. Beah has a bachelor's degree in political science from Oberlin College and lives in New York City.

Child rights:
On the right path,
but a long way to go

by Ishmael Beah

The remarkable value of the Convention on the Rights of the Child may not always be fully appreciated in countries where child rights are not systemically threatened or abused. I came to understand the need for a specific, legally binding international instrument addressing child rights after living in Sierra Leone, a country that for many years was consumed by fear, death and the violation of human rights. As a child growing up during the civil war, I was forced to fight in the conflict that ravaged the social fabric of my home and society. Human rights violations were rampant, but through the work of organizations committed to the implementation of the Convention I was eventually freed from my involvement in the war. Later, after leaving Sierra Leone, I began working as an advocate for children affected by armed conflict. The Convention and its two Optional Protocols have become valuable tools for me in creating a strong advocacy platform to speak on the rights of children.

My introduction to the Convention occurred in the winter of 1996, during my first trip to the United States. I came to the United Nations to attend a conference organized by UNICEF and Norwegian People's Aid on the effect of war on children. This conference recognized the importance of including children in discussions of their rights and incorporated many of the principles identified in the groundbreaking Machel study on the impact of armed conflict on children launched that year.

During the conference I met 56 other children who had been directly impacted by armed conflict and who, like me, were being introduced to the child rights articulated by the Convention. I was 16 years old at the time, and I remember how this knowledge – particularly for those of us from war-torn countries – rekindled the value of our lives and our humanity. In that moment, I knew I would work as an advocate for children's rights, and my commitment to spread awareness on the Convention was born.

Before the Convention gained widespread acceptance in the 1990s, it was difficult and extremely rare for there to be public discussions about child rights. While there is undoubtedly much to be done in ensuring widespread implementation of the Convention, its entry into force has set the stage for the application of national-level monitoring and accountability mechanisms. The incorporation of many of the Convention's articles and principles into national legal structures gives children and youth hope that one day their rights will be realized. During my travels throughout the world, I have seen that once children know these rights exist, they eagerly ask for them to be met, and they have expressed the value of having a common legal standard. Knowledge of the Convention's existence enables them to ask their governments to provide for their rights in concrete terms.

The Convention consists of 54 articles that encompass a broad range of economic, social, civil, cultural and political rights, all of which contribute to creating a powerful and com-

The incorporation of many of the Convention's articles and principles into national legal structures gives children and youth hope that one day their rights will be realized.

prehensive framework for child rights. My experiences, first as a child realizing my rights had been violated and now as an advocate for child rights, have convinced me there are specific articles that set a baseline of responsibility from which the other articles operate.

The first of these is article 6, which states that all governments must "ensure to the maximum extent possible the survival and development of the child." In places where human rights are not guaranteed, article 6 serves as a tool for lobbying on behalf of children, to remove them from war and to protect them from harm. It also provides a mandate to safeguard the development of children, which in war-torn countries often requires the presence and efforts of human rights workers. I benefited from the existence of aid workers in Sierra Leone, and from the rights embodied in this article.

My life has also been enriched by articles 12 and 13, which guarantee children and youth the right to express their views fully in matters affecting them, and "to seek, receive and impart important information" of all kinds and by all media. These articles have helped many children become active participants in finding solutions to problems that affect them. By encouraging children and youth to be outspoken through artistic mediums, and by including them on government and United Nations panels, officials are moving from looking at children's rights in abstract terms to seeing them as the deeply human struggles they are.

Articles 28 and 29, which articulate the right to education, also require special mention. In post-conflict nations, where refugees and internally displaced persons are struggling to rebuild their lives, children fiercely want an education. When children and youth engage in school, or informal learning, the chances of them being recruited for war or violence, for hard labour or exploitation lessen. Lack of education is a root cause of many of the injustices children suffer, and more must be done to provide them with access to quality schools. This is particularly true for young girls, who often suffer the additional burdens of domestic labour, child marriage and early pregnancy, sexual violence and gender-based discrimination.

The work to fulfil child rights is not an easy task. But it is one that cannot be ignored. The Convention on the Rights of the Child demands that families, communities and governments acknowledge and meet their fundamental responsibilities to care for and protect the world's 2.2 billion children. While I believe the international community has come a long way in the implementation of the Convention, stronger child, youth and community participation is required to sustain success. Ultimately, children will determine the moral and ethical future of nations, and the world. Their voices must be heard.

©UNICEF/HQ08-0823/John Isaac

Grade 4 students hold 'Window of Hope' certificates at the end of a life-skills education session at Ehenya Primary School in the northern Oshana Region, Namibia.

Tan Sri Dato Muhyiddin Mohd Yassin is the Deputy Prime Minister and Minister of Education of Malaysia. A father of four, Minister Yassin previously served as the Minister of Youth and Sports. He is committed to ensuring students in Malaysia receive a well-rounded education that blends classroom learning with extra-curricular and sporting activities.

Reaching the unreached in Malaysia through education

by Tan Sri Dato Muhyiddin Mohd Yassin

The desire to attain the best education in life is a common aspiration that binds all people together. Education is a universal dream, one that grants transformative seeds of opportunity to every child. It is the dream of a young girl who pores over her books by candlelight and carefully tucks them into her bag for school the next day. It is the dream of a little boy who falls asleep to the humming rhythm of a city, and the same dream of children who wake up to the sound of boats returning from the early morning catch.

In Malaysia today, children and adults enjoy access to education as part of the legacy formed more than 50 years ago by the founders of our country. Shortly after independence, the Government passed the 1952 Education Ordinance, resolving to honour education as a basic right. This legislation laid the groundwork for strong government commitment to investing in education, which was further enhanced by the country's ratification of the Convention on the Rights of the Child, in 1995. Learning in Malaysia was democratized, ensuring that all children have the right to schooling, regardless of their sex, social or economic background, resident or HIV status. By providing free and compulsory primary education, as well as 11 years of universal education, we are turning the spirit of the Convention into a reality.

Our forefathers recognized the singular importance of quality education in meeting the development needs of the country, and shaped their policies around the idea that when every child has an education the entire nation prospers. By committing continuous and substantial government expenditure to education, we have worked tirelessly to lift children out of the shadows of disparity.

Public investment in schools has been a key factor in successfully reducing poverty from the high levels seen in the 1970s to the negligible level prevalent today. In 1970, one third of Malaysia's population aged six and over had never attended school. Today, Malaysia is close to achieving the second Millennium Development Goal of universal primary education, with almost all school-age children completing six years of learning.

Likewise, the Government has worked towards ending gender disparity by ensuring that women have access not only to school but also to the full range of business and political employment enjoyed by their male counterparts. These efforts complement the Convention's vision that every child's individual personality, talents and abilities should be developed to the fullest.

Our goals in meeting the requirements of the Convention are to provide equity in education, regardless of whether a child is from a minority group, has special needs or comes from a vulnerable community. One way we are contributing to this effort is to ensure that parents and families have resources to enable their children's full engagement in school. Poorer families are assisted through support programmes that help with uniforms and shoes, scholarships, textbook loan schemes, tuition vouchers, supplementary feeding and school milk programmes, school health facilities and residential schools.

By committing continuous and substantial government expenditure on education, we have worked tirelessly to lift children out of the shadows of disparity.

While we have made great progress in achieving universal enrolment, the more elusive challenge now facing the country is guaranteeing access to quality education for the most vulnerable children. In addition to building classrooms and putting children in them, educating disenfranchised children requires identifying disparities in children's abilities and socioeconomic status. Addressing these concerns involves acknowledging the importance of self-accessed, self-directed and self-paced learning.

Malaysia is charting a new path by using information and communication technology (ICT) to make education relevant and attractive in an increasingly globalized world. More than half of all schools across Malaysia currently have computer labs and nearly every school is equipped with Internet access, courtesy of the Government's SchoolNet project.

Children collaborate on a project using a minicomputer at Timbang Island Primary School, on Timbang Island in the state of Sabah, Malaysia.

Developing ICT infrastructure, however, is only the first step. Our broader vision is to awaken and nurture the desire for 21st century knowledge and skills, and to transform the education system towards a 'Smart School' model that utilizes technology in learning. We are integrating this approach into a student-centred system that stimulates thinking, creativity and caring by teaching ICT literacy in primary and secondary schools. Additionally, we have introduced holistic education through 88 pilot Smart Schools and by equipping special-needs schools with computers and courseware for the hearing and vision impaired.

The endeavour for technologically advanced education is not without its challenges, and staying on the forefront of infrastructure development and cutting-edge technology, as well as providing access and equity to advanced learning tools, requires significant resources. One method for overcoming these hurdles is through strategic partnerships with the private sector. These collaborations not only engage the community but also create exciting opportunities for students to expand their horizons beyond traditional academic offerings.

One such project the Government has undertaken involves working with Malaysia's first cable TV provider, Astro, to bring the world to children living in the remotest interiors of East Malaysia. With this partnership, we are beaming learning content through satellites and giving these children the opportunity to interact with science and technology through mobile learning trucks.

As the world grows increasingly connected by technology and the transfer of ideas, comprehensive education is becoming a reality for children across the globe. But much remains to be done to ensure that regardless of age, sex, race, ethnic origin or socioeconomic status, all children are given the opportunity to learn.

In Malaysia, education is no longer a distant dream, but a promise we have made to every child. Drawing on the Convention on the Rights of the Child, we will press on in our efforts to care for the most vulnerable and isolated of children. Our hope is to build a better future for the children of our country and, in turn, to see them build a better future for our world.

Participation and compliance: The Committee on the Rights of the Child

by Yanghee Lee

*Professor **Yanghee Lee** is the current Chairperson of the Committee on the Rights of the Child. She has been a member of the Committee since 2003 and was elected as its Chair in both May of 2007 and 2009. A national of the Republic of Korea, Professor Lee has taught at Sungkyunkwan University since 1991. She is the recipient of many recognitions and awards, including the 2007 Year of the Woman Award (Korea).*

This is a landmark year for children and all who work alongside them and on their behalf as we celebrate the 50th anniversary of the Declaration of the Rights of the Child and the 20th anniversary of the Convention on the Rights of the Child. As a legally binding document, the Convention has been instrumental in setting standards of children's rights and motivating institutional capacity-building for the promotion and protection of children. It has made children and their claim as equal participants in societies more visible by calling for their inclusion in public and political discourses on issues affecting them. Since its inception, many countries have undertaken legislative reforms to include children's rights in their constitutions.

Compliance with the Convention has not been without its challenges. That children are true and deserving rights holders is not an easy concept for many societies around the world to accept. Likewise, the justiciability of the rights enshrined in the Convention continues to be debated. Despite these challenges, its success is undeniable. On the Convention's 20th anniversary, it is important to celebrate the many ways it has advanced children's rights while also acknowledging that it will have to adapt to a new century of threats facing children.

One of the more effective implementation measures of the Convention was the creation of an independent body of experts that reviews the integration of the Convention into international jurisprudence and States' national systems. The Committee on the Rights of the Child met for the first time in 1991, and as of its 51st session 18 years later has reviewed 333 country reports on compliance to the Convention, 47 country reports on compliance to the Optional Protocol on the involvement of children in armed conflict and 35 country reports on compliance to the Optional Protocol on the sale of children, child prostitution and child pornography.

The Convention and the Committee continue to be vital in the initiation of critically important international activities regarding child rights. Once a year, the Committee holds a Day of General Discussion that is devoted to in-depth analysis of an area of children's rights. This practice started in 1992 with an exploration of children in armed conflict and ultimately resulted in the Secretary-General commissioning a major study on the impact of armed conflict on children. This produced the groundbreaking report by Graça Machel that has revolutionized the way the United Nations and the governments of its Member States respond to the mobilization of resources to children in conflict zones. Likewise, the UN Study on Violence against Children, which revealed the magnitude and degree of violence that children around the world are subjected to, was inspired by a Day of General Discussion.

The Committee also releases General Comments that are its interpretation of a particular right or theme enshrined in the Convention. These functions provide guidance to States

We must continue to work to ensure the dignity of children is preserved and hold States accountable to define their obligations, both in material and moral terms, to prevent violations of children's rights.

parties on their responsibilities under the Convention while helping to bolster its compliance. One of the most influential comments to date is General Comment No. 5, which identifies several ways States parties should understand and implement the Convention. This comment has provoked challenges to governments to enshrine child rights and protection into their existing national systems. Since its publication, many countries have begun to withdraw reservations to the Convention, set up coordinating bodies and ombudsperson offices that specifically advocate for and administer policies for children and include them in the decision-making process.

Boys carry a banner advocating children's rights and opposing sexual abuse during a march celebrating the Day of the African Child in Juba, capital of Southern Sudan.

The most recent interpretation of the human rights provisions enshrined in the Convention is General Comment No. 12 (2009) on the right of the child to be heard. The Convention itself does not specifically mention the right to participate, but Article 12, which is addressed in this General Comment, has come to be known as the 'participation right'. With the publication of this General Comment, the third 'P' – of provision, protection and participation – is strengthened, giving full recognition to children as rights holders.

The call for greater participation by children is gaining additional momentum from an initiative brought by Slovenia and advanced by Slovakia earlier this year. The Human Rights Council unanimously agreed to establish an open-ended working group to explore the adoption of a third Optional Protocol to the Convention. This protocol would provide a communications procedure allowing children and other child rights stakeholders to air grievances to the Committee and challenge abuses of their rights. More than 38 Member States co-sponsored the creation of this group, which is to have its first session in Geneva before the end of 2009. Regardless of the group's decisions and recommendations, its very creation signals the seriousness with which States parties take children's rights.

This fall, the Committee on the Rights of the Child will spend focused energy analysing the challenges, old and new, that confront the realization of children's rights. After 193 ratifications and 19 years of reporting, the need for a robust evaluation and analysis mechanism to better understand the situation of children is more important than ever. We must continue to work to ensure the dignity of children is preserved and hold States accountable for defining their obligations, both in material and moral terms, to prevent violations of children's rights. This includes challenging societies to address the many and varied ways they commodify children and the associated discrimination that does not view children as legitimate rights holders. States parties must include children in the policymaking process and ensure their voices are heard and considered in the development of programmes and standards that uniquely impact their lives. Only when States embrace children as their partners will their rights take root and later bear the fruit of peace and equality the Convention seeks for each child. Members of the Committee join the community of nations and individuals worldwide that in celebrating children's rights and the 20th anniversary of the Convention.

A movement of the heart: Promoting the value of children with intellectual disabilities

by Timothy P. Shriver

Timothy P. Shriver is the Chairman and CEO of Special Olympics. Before assuming this leadership position, he worked as an educator focusing on the social and emotional factors of learning. His work in substance abuse, violence, dropout and teen pregnancy prevention led to the creation of the New Haven Public Schools' Social Development Project, considered the leading school-based prevention effort in the United States. He is a member of the Council on Foreign Relations.

Twenty years ago, the Convention on the Rights of the Child broke new ground for children's rights, empowerment and dignity around the world. Since then, its position on children's rights has prompted a broad rethinking of how children are viewed, valued and treated. It may seem obvious now, but the Convention was the first international document to argue that children are important and have intrinsic human rights.

Two decades before the Convention's adoption, a small movement was born with values similar to those that would eventually be embodied in the treaty. On playing fields around the world, the Special Olympics welcomed children and adults with intellectual disabilities to train and compete in sports with a simple message: People with intellectual disabilities matter too.

For 40 years, Special Olympics has used sports as a catalyst for the health and empowerment of individuals with intellectual disabilities and the transformation of communities. Today, over 3 million athletes participate in more than 30,000 events each year. Every time athletes with intellectual disabilities defy society's low expectations and assume the mantle of champions, they make a claim not only for their athletic achievement but also for their humanity.

Sadly, for most children with intellectual disabilities, the full life promised by the Convention remains out of reach. Although nearly all of the world's countries have adopted the treaty, by and large, its core principles have yet to be assimilated by communities and societies. Attitudes towards people with intellectual disabilities remain negative and corrosive. Institutional care persists as a primary care model, and in many cases, it is subhuman. Education and employment opportunities remain limited.

On the 20th anniversary of the Convention, it is imperative for governments and individual citizens to press for a revitalized effort for its implementation around the world. I believe a new model of engagement – one that goes beyond legal frameworks to create a social movement – is necessary. Governments alone cannot do all the necessary work to change communities. While it is one thing to set a standard in law, it is quite another to set a standard in people's hearts. The true fulfilment of the Convention will only come when children with intellectual disabilities, along with other children who face marginalization and discrimination, are treated with dignity and justice not just in writing but also in daily life.

This will not be easy. First, there is the glaring problem of translating the language of human rights into a movement of change for people with intellectual disabilities. Far too often, the subtle devaluation of children with intellectual disabilities creeps in, and transgressions against their dignity are overlooked. These children need a different view of

The future of rights for people with intellectual disabilities requires a new, positive message in which we all own the rights agenda.

rights precisely because their claim to self-worth and justice transcends their ability to advocate for themselves against entrenched discrimination.

In addition to re-conceptualizing rights for children with disabilities, there is an urgent need for individuals and communities to become strong advocates for the Convention. When rights are defined only by political or judicial norms, they do very little to advance a cause whose barriers are social and cultural. The future of rights for people with intellectual disabilities requires a new, positive message in which we all own the rights agenda. Without individuals becoming partners in the Convention, change will remain far off.

I have heard countless stories of the discrimination and stigma that are too often directed at children with intellectual disabilities. Taunts like 'retard' are hurled across schoolyards, dinner tables and street corners, leaving in their wake children in heartbreaking tears and desperate loneliness. Around the world, unknown numbers of children sit on concrete floors in dark institutions, sentenced to a prison of isolation. In every country, legions of parents can recount instances when they were advised to be ashamed of their own children. I am repeatedly told reasons why this occurs, and why it is unrealistic to accord children with intellectual disabilities a welcome. There are many reasons indeed. But there is no good reason.

A yound girl and therapist at Dar el Hanan (House of Mercy) centre for disabled children in Alexandria, Egypt.

© UNICEF/NYHQ1996-1055/Toutounji

The child rights movement we need will be a movement of the heart. It will not be for children with intellectual disabilities; it will be led with them. It will engage billions of people in overturning the language of exclusion, in appreciating the diversity of the human family, in recognizing the beauty of each child. It will make basic education a right for every child. It will replace words like 'disability' with new constructs such as 'diffability' that celebrate the differences we all carry through life.

In the end, the child rights movement of the heart may become the most powerful legacy of the Convention. Through its decades of drafting and eventual adoption, the Convention marked a first in history – a moment when the community of nations acknowledged the dignity and intrinsic worth of all children. It will be fulfilled with another first – the moment when communities of citizens celebrate the value of every child with no exceptions or limits. When this happens, the age-old saying will be fulfilled: The stone the builders rejected has become the cornerstone, and it is marvelous to behold.

*Awa N'deye Ouedraogo
is a former member
and Chair of the UN
Committee on the Rights
of the Child. She has
served extensively as
an adviser for both the
United Nations and the
Government of Burkina
Faso. Ms. Ouedraogo
holds an advanced degree
in linguistic studies from
the Sorbonne.*

Ending child trafficking:
Collaboration is key

by Awa N'deye Ouedraogo

The United Nations Convention on the Rights of the Child was the first international human rights agreement to explicitly protect children. The need for a legal acknowledgement of children's rights is so well agreed by States that, despite its relatively young age, the Convention is the most widely ratified international document in existence. Over the 20 years since its adoption by the UN General Assembly, the Convention itself has 'grown up' and, as the concept of child rights has solidified, the need to protect youth and adolescents has been increasingly recognized by governments and local and international organizations.

Greater recognition of the critical importance of child protection has resulted in the addition of two Optional Protocols to the Convention, enhanced monitoring of child rights, and the integration of the Convention into national legal systems. As we celebrate the 20th anniversary of the Convention, it is time to reflect on the changes it has engendered in the day-to-day lives of children throughout the world.

Implementation of the Convention is monitored by the Committee on the Rights of the Child. All States parties to the Convention are obliged to present reports to the Committee every five years, allowing it to analyse the treatment of children in their countries. Since the establishment of the Committee, which I chaired from 2000 to 2001, reports submitted by governments have shown that the Convention has generated positive and sustainable changes in the lives of many children in the world.

The Committee has found that, since the Convention's entry into force, large numbers of children now know that they have rights. This has allowed them to raise awareness about children's issues among their peers, parents and communities. Many of these children also understand how to claim their rights, and how to use this knowledge to combat maltreatment, exploitation and gender discrimination.

It is my experience that the Convention is the most important tool in protecting vulnerable children from a broad spectrum of political, social and economic injustices. In addition to increasing youth involvement in claiming their own rights, the Convention has also enabled States parties to provide funding and programmes that focus on youth and adolescents. These efforts have resulted in the successful development of initiatives ranging from immunization programmes to providing specialized treatment for children living with HIV, education and health services, and improving access to water and sanitation supplies. Through these efforts, the physical well-being of children is enhanced, allowing for an increased focus on their mental, spiritual and emotional growth.

The Convention has resulted in measurable improvement in the treatment of the world's children, but there are several areas of child rights where much remains to be done. One

It is my experience that the Convention is the most important tool in protecting vulnerable children from a broad spectrum of political, social and economic injustices.

critical issue is child trafficking – a gross violation of human rights that affects an estimated 1.2 million children every year. Traffickers take disadvantaged children from their families, often with the consent of parents, who unknowingly agree to uncertain promises in attempts to secure better futures for their children. Once children are caught in traffickers' nets, they are exposed to severe abuses, exploitation and violations of their fundamental human rights. They lack legal protection, and the separation from their families makes them extremely vulnerable to being forced into child marriage, prostitution, labour or armed conflict.

Conscious of the existence of these abuses, concerned governments are adopting measures to prevent and combat child trafficking. Unfortunately, these laws and policies have been unsuccessful in eliminating the practice. Traffickers are often aware of governments' anti-trafficking efforts, and, in countries where they are enforced, the traffickers are able to circumvent them. A further tragedy of trafficking is that rescued children do not receive care and treatment that is sufficient or appropriate. They are normally sent back to their families without having been rehabilitated from their traumatic experiences, and may face stigma, discrimination, rejection and ostracism when they return home.

© UNICEF/NYHQ2007-1671/Giacomo Pirozzi

Government officials participate in a training session on the prevention of child trafficking at the Tihama Development Authority in the town of Hodeidah, Yemen.

While many States parties have signed bilateral and regional agreements to combat child trafficking, these instruments lack proper monitoring and evaluation systems. Furthermore, without addressing poverty and unemployment, programmes to end trafficking will only provide short-term solutions to the exploitation of these children. To better combat child trafficking, governments should build on the legal and social mandates of the Convention, and review legislation with a comprehensive view to banning the practice.

Additionally, information and sensitization programmes on the existence of child trafficking need to be directed towards the general public, with a special emphasis on educating vulnerable children. Perpetrators of trafficking must be swiftly punished, signalling to those who may abuse children that the world's governments take the issue of child protection seriously. By creating a holistic strategy to reduce and eliminate poverty, countries can also address the social determinants of trafficking and other forms of violence against children.

On the 20th anniversary of the Convention on the Rights of the Child, I launch an urgent appeal to all governments facing child trafficking to undertake bold and coordinated actions at national and international levels to put an end to the exploitation of the world's children. The continued practice of child trafficking is compromising the promotion of child rights and is undermining the achievements made since the Convention was ratified. It is my hope that through the combined efforts of governments, international organizations and individual citizens, genuine and effective promotion of child rights will be realized and child trafficking will be ended.

Putting children at the heart of the European Union

A comprehensive strategy on children's rights

The promotion of children's rights is a key priority for me as a European Commissioner. Living up to the challenge of supporting children in developing to their full potential is an objective close to my heart. The Commission's Communication 'Towards an EU Strategy on the Rights of the Child' has proposed the establishment of a comprehensive strategy to safeguard children's rights in its internal and external policies.

Concrete steps are being taken to improve the protection of children from all types of violence and quickly adapt to new threats emerging from modern technology, including a European-wide hotline number for missing children – 116 000. Children now face dangers, such as cyberbullying and manipulation from online predators, that did not previously exist. Earlier this year, I proposed two legislative measures to strengthen the fight against human trafficking, sexual exploitation of children and child pornography that take these risks into account.

The proposals aim to prevent repeat sex offenders by improving cooperation between Member States, so that offenders prosecuted in one are barred from engaging in professions involving children in another. Moreover, they should facilitate tougher sanctions against perpetrators, allow child victims to testify in court without facing their abusers and reinforce the need for cooperation between civil society, governments and national criminal justice authorities.

The 20th anniversary of the Convention is an opportunity for us to renew our commitment to act together to protect our children from all kinds of threats so they can become the future architects of our democracies.

The ideal gift

The ideal gift to commemorate the 20th anniversary of the Convention on the Rights of the Child would be for the European Community to sign the Convention as a concrete expression of its commitment to children's rights. Unfortunately, the Convention does not permit signing by regional bodies. Despite this limitation, the EU *de facto* respects the Convention's authority.

The EU's challenge is to fulfil its declared intent so children are not an afterthought in development and humanitarian work. As the biggest provider of development aid in the world, Europe can drive this change. The EU promotes several policies on children's rights that contribute to the fulfilment of the Convention, including an integrated human rights-based approach that emphasizes the importance of basic services and child protection systems.

Given the current global financial crisis, which has put the prosperity of future generations at risk, it is more relevant than ever to put children at the forefront of our partner relationships. History shows that children are especially vulnerable to recessions, as they are often removed from school to work or suffer malnutrition as food becomes scarce. This can have a permanent impact on children's development, with important future implications for society as a whole. The EU is keen to help our partners respond to this crisis by ensuring they maintain their social services spending.

We are starting to see progress on children's rights, and I hope that on the Convention's 20th anniversary, these efforts will bear further fruit.

JACQUES BARROT
Vice-President of the European Commission, European Commissioner for Justice, Freedom and Security

LOUIS MICHEL
European Commissioner for Development and Humanitarian Aid

JAVIER SOLANA

High Representative for the Common Foreign and Security Policy, Secretary-General of the Council of the European Union

BENITA FERRERO-WALDNER

European Commissioner for External Relations and the European Neighbourhood Policy

Building stronger children, building stronger societies

The Convention on the Rights of the Child brought about a new vision of children, recognizing that they require distinct attention and are neither the property of their parents nor helpless objects of charity. Rather, the Convention identifies them as human beings with their own rights.

The Convention has played a major role in catalysing child-specific policies at domestic, regional and international levels. It has been a key source of inspiration for the European Union. The EU Charter of Fundamental Rights explicitly recognizes children's rights and reaffirms the EC's obligations to act in children's best interests and to take their views into account. In 2003, the EU adopted 'Guidelines on Children and Armed Conflict' to address the short, medium and long-term impact of armed conflict on children. The 2007 EU 'Guidelines for the Promotion and Protection of the Rights of the Child' affirm the EU's determination to consider the promotion and protection of children's rights as a matter of priority in its external human rights policy.

Despite these and other accomplishments much remains to be done. I firmly believe that by investing in children we lay the foundation for a world where passivity and indifference to human rights violations have no place. The normative and ethical framework of the Convention is a strong foundation for the way forward. We know that by enabling children to participate, we are contributing to building stronger children, and that stronger children will be able to build stronger societies – and ultimately a better world.

Where they should be: Putting children high on the political agenda

I believe a key impact of the Convention has been to get international actors – including the European Union – to put children's rights high on their political agendas. Europe has a strong commitment to children's rights, but progress at the political level must be supplemented by concrete action. The EU has a long record of delivering support to children – from building schools in Gaza to providing relief in emergency situations in Sri Lanka.

The EU operates on the same principles as the Convention. I see the great benefit of having a clear, internationally recognized and binding framework that helps us work with partner countries to alleviate the suffering of children who have no access to clean water or sanitation, education, or who live in conflict zones.

But there is a great deal left to do. Making children's participation a reality is a key challenge. EU officials recently conveyed to me how rewarding they find work with children, which provides an opportunity to include children in discussions about their rights on equal footing. Listening to children allows us to empower them. I believe this is something we all can do better: involving children in dialogues about the policies that affect them.

The 20th anniversary of the Convention on the Rights of the Child is an opportunity to renew our commitment to those at the heart of our efforts – children everywhere – and to vow that we will not rest until all children around the world are fully enjoying their rights.

The full version of each European Union Commissioner's essay is available on the UNICEF website at <www.unicef.org/rightsite>.

Challenges for the Convention in the 21st century

As the first decade of the 21st century draws to a close, the Convention on the Rights of the Child stands at a pivotal moment. Despite its pervasive influence and the many achievements in child rights that have resulted since its adoption, hundreds of millions of children still remain excluded from the essential services and care, protection and participation that are their right.

It does not have to be this way, however. Even in the midst of the worst global economic crisis in 80 years, and at a moment when climate change is beginning to threaten livelihoods and survival throughout the developing world, opportunities to advance child rights abound. They are evident in the many initiatives and programmes promoting child rights around the world, and in the increased investment and greater collaboration in primary health care, education and protection of recent years.

The great challenge for the next 20 years will be to unite governmental accountability for child rights with social, institutional and individual participation, expanding responsibility for the implementation of the Convention from the States parties that signed and ratified it to the broad stakeholders that they represent. To make the vision of the Convention a reality for every child, it must, in effect, become a guiding document for every human being.

UNICEF/NYHQ2008-1277/Josh Estey

Economic, climate and population shifts threaten recent advances in child rights

The Convention on the Rights of the Child turns 20 at a volatile time. The year 2009 has been marked by the worst global financial crisis since the Great Depression 80 years ago. Banking bailout, monetary policy responses and fiscal stimulus packages in industrialized and developing countries alike are attempting to restore solvency to the international financial sector, underpin macroeconomic stability and set the basis for recovery in 2010 and beyond. But, as this report goes to press in mid-2009, the world economic outlook remains highly uncertain.

> The risks to child rights from the current economic crisis and other external challenges must not be underestimated.

The international economic context is important for child rights, because it forms an integral part of the external environment that influences the actions of all those entrusted with the care and protection of children. Strains on household, corporate and government budgets are threatening spending on services and commodities essential to meeting children's rights to survival, development, protection and participation.

Add the sharp spikes in food and fuel prices of 2008, the steep rise in unemployment and the precipitous fall in world output, trade and investment this year, and it is easy to understand the pressures on families and communities and the concomitant risks to children's education, nutritional status and health care – to name but three aspects of child rights – particularly among the least developed countries and the poorest and most vulnerable communities and social groups in all nations (see Panel on *The global economic crisis: Implications for child rights*, page 62).

The current turmoil will not threaten all the child rights gains of the past two decades. For the individuals who have benefited from them, some advances are largely irreversible. For example, a child who has received a quality primary education and gone on to secondary education has already acquired knowledge and competencies that will last a life-time. A young person who has been immunized in childhood will enjoy longstanding, often lifelong, protection from major diseases.

However, while the health and education gains may be permanent for the current generation of beneficiaries, the services on which they depend are far more vulnerable to changing economic conditions. Sustaining quality education requires continued investment in schools, curricula and teachers. Maintaining levels of immunization and other basic health-care services necessitates large-scale outlays in procurement and distribution. Supporting environmental health depends on expanding and upgrading water and sanitation facilities.

Combating HIV and AIDS, malaria, tuberculosis and other major infectious diseases and conditions demands ongoing investments in preventive and curative interventions. Creating national child protection systems implies intensifying the recruitment, training and supervising of specialized professionals. All of these services will require far greater levels of commitment and investment than pre-crisis levels if the Millennium Development Goals are to be met on time and the World Fit for Children compact is to be fulfilled.

The challenges for child rights come not only from the economic sphere. Demographic shifts are set to alter the regional distribution of the world's children over the next two decades. Consider one sobering fact: By 2030, 40 years after the Convention's entry into force, one quarter of the world's under-fives will live in the 49 countries currently considered as least developed, compared to roughly 14 per cent in 1990.[1] This increase will place even greater pressure on the governments of those countries to fulfil the rights of their youngest citizens through expanded investment in quality maternal, neonatal and child nutrition and health care, early childhood development programmes and measures to protect young children against violence and abuse. Without far greater efforts to reach children in the most marginalized and impoverished areas, the risk is high that this quartile of the world's youngest citizens will face even greater relative disparities in access to health care, education and protection than faced by their current counterparts in the poorest nations.

They may also face an increasingly inhospitable natural environment. Growing evidence of the impact and extent of climate change suggests that damage to the environment may threaten such hard-won advances as improved drinking water, greater food security, lower undernutrition among under-fives and stronger disease control in many developing countries. These countries – which are located mostly in

© UNICEF/NYHQ2008-0930/Nicole Toutounji

Daniela Melendez, 14, Colombia

Climate change poses a risk to gains in child survival and development achieved in the past two decades. Children should be key contributors and partners in strategies for adaptation and mitigation. *A 14–year-old artist, from Colombia, at 'Paint for the Planet', a children's art exhibit held at UN headquarters in October 2008 to launch the global 'UNite to Combat Climate Change' campaign.*

warmer regions and whose source of external trade income derives mainly from primary commodities – may be the worst affected by changes in rainfall patterns, greater weather extremes and increasing droughts and floods. The increased number and severity of natural disasters in recent years, and deteriorating conditions in several areas experiencing protracted emergencies, particularly sub-Saharan Africa, are signs that humanitarian crises – known to affect children and women disproportionately – are on the rise[2] (see Panel on *Protecting children's rights in humanitarian crises,* page 63). These external challenges will complicate the task of fulfilling the child rights agenda outlined in Chapter I of this report and articulated by guest contributors in Chapter II.

The risks to child rights from the current economic crisis and other challenges from the external environment must not be underestimated. Experience and research indicate that children and women are highly vulnerable to economic, demographic and climatic shifts; for children, in particular, the repercussions of these shocks can have lifelong consequences that may span generations and undermine efforts to advance child rights in the next two decades unless action is taken.

But while history underscores these risks, it also shows that crises can also present opportunities for advancing child rights and well-being. The child rights movement emerged from the shadow of World War I, led by the pioneering efforts of Eglantyne Jebb and Save the Children International. UNICEF itself was born from the ashes of World War II, providing the United Nations with an international organization dedicated to the survival and care of children. Despite the oil price shock that shook the world economy in 1973 and the accompanying global stock market crash that extended into 1974, the latter year also saw the launch of the most successful public health initiative of all time: the Expanded Programme on Immunization, which has saved millions of lives over the past 35 years.[3] Latin American countries made some of their strongest gains in child survival during the 'lost decade' of the 1980s. During the 1990s and early 2000s, several emerging markets – including Argentina, Brazil, the Republic of Korea and Turkey – experienced liquidity crises while sustaining gains in education and health care from earlier years.[4]

Innovative efforts to protect and educate children in such complex emergencies as the 2004 Indian Ocean tsunami, extreme violence in Darfur and the emergency in Afghanistan are more recent examples of successful initiatives that have enhanced child rights in times of crisis – sometimes enabling children to fulfil their rights to these

The global economic crisis: Implications for child rights

History has shown that children and women are particularly vulnerable to economic turmoil. Financial and economic shocks in developing countries prior to the 2008–2009 global economic crisis have led to higher under-five mortality rates, lower school enrolment, rising insecurity and children forced to work in dangerous environments. Reductions in public expenditure on health and education have driven children and their families into poverty traps that are not easily escaped once the crisis has passed.

There have been growing concerns that the 2008–2009 global economic crisis, compounded by recent food and fuel price instability, could result in rising poverty and undernutrition in developing countries. As this report goes to press in August 2009, the global economic outlook remains exceptionally uncertain, despite signs of improving forward-looking economic indicators in recent months.

The full impact of the crisis on child rights will not be evident for some time, and will only become apparent as new international estimates of global poverty, child development and nutrition emerge. Appropriate policy responses are required to protect child and families from the consequences economic crises.

Ensure adequate nutrition for families. Although international food prices have declined since peaking in 2008, they remain high relative to their long-term trends. In many developing countries, domestic food prices remain far above historical levels. Measures to safeguard the nutritional status of families in times of economic crisis include direct supplementation measures – such as therapeutic foods for young children – and supporting measures to ensure access to essential micronutrients, improved environmental health facilities, quality healthcare, and

promote best practices for hygiene, food preparation and storage. Nutrition monitoring should also include appraisal of the direct and underlying factors determining child growth and nutrition.

Protect budgets for essential services. Safeguarding, and even increasing, social budgets should be an integral component of countries' responses to shocks. Missing the window of opportunity to invest in children has clear adverse implications for children's survival and development prospects. It can also limit a nation's future growth potential. Analysis of data from 120 developing countries for the period 1975–2000 indicates that increasing education spending as share of gross domestic product by 1 per cent over a 15 year period could lead to universal primary school enrolment, while reducing the poverty headcount by around 17 per cent.

Invest in child-sensitive social protection. Effective and comprehensive social protection programmes can ameliorate the negative impact of economic crises on poor families. In response to the 1997 Asian financial crisis, which followed a severe drought in the region, the governments of Indonesia, the Philippines and Thailand implemented or strengthened nutrition programmes for children and bolstered access to education by providing scholarships and funding allocations and undertaking community awareness campaigns. During its 2002 debt crisis, Argentina sought to protect poor households from the worst effects by providing income support to unemployed heads of household; this initiative is estimate to have prevented an additional 10 per cent of participating families from falling below the food poverty line and lowered the incidence of extreme poverty across the nation. Renowned and ongoing social protection

initiatives in Mexico (Oportunidades) and Brazil (Programa Saude da Family) have resulted in falling infant mortality rates and lower rates of poverty.

Despite the well-documented merits of social protection programmes, many developing countries do not have such systems in place. According to recent research surveying 144 developing countries, 19 of 49 low-income countries and 49 of 95 middle-income countries have no social safety net programmes, and only one third of all countries surveyed had some form of cash transfers.

Limit the additional demands on women and girls. Empowering women to become key household decision-makers and ensuring that girls and young women have access to quality education and healthcare is pivotal to making social protection effective. Declining government spending on education and health associated with economic crises can transfer the burden of service provision on households and communities, adding to the already high demands on women and girls. Women and girls also bear the brunt of coping mechanisms, including reduced spending on such essential services and commodities as food, fuel, education and health care, and increased time spent on activities that either save or generate additional income.

Ensuring the rights of children in the current economic crisis and the recovery period that follows requires making difficult but decisive choices. For the crisis not to leave a legacy of deprivation for generations, the choice has to be to safeguard, support, and if possible, expand, the essential services, protection and participation that are the right of all children at all times.

See References, pages 90–92.

Protecting children's rights in humanitarian crises

Humanitarian crises, including natural disasters and complex emergencies, compromise children's rights to survival, development, protection and participation. Complex emergencies can undermine primary health care systems and physical infrastructure, jeopardising child nutrition and health. Education, too, suffers; of the estimated 101 million children of primary school age not attending primary school, nearly 60 million live in the 33 countries currently affected by armed conflict.

The disruption to the social order caused by emergencies heightens the potential for women and children to be exploited for economic and sexual purposes. Sexual violence may occur as a byproduct of the social disruption or may actually be employed as a weapon of war, and can leave its survivors with severe and long-lasting trauma, sexually-transmitted diseases and unwanted pregnancies. Recent studies in the Democratic Republic of the Congo and northern Uganda found that children born from sexual violence are often identified with the perpetrator and consequently discriminated against or neglected.

The changing environment for humanitarian action

In the two decades since the Convention was adopted, the landscape in which humanitarian action takes place has evolved. Climate change and the burgeoning global population are increasing competition for limited resources, including access to water, and raising concerns about food security. Conflicts are increasingly characterized by protracted intra-state hostility, with a significant impact on civilians, including extensive internal displacement. About 50 per cent of the estimated 26 million people currently displaced by armed conflicts and violence are children. Disregard for the protected status of civilians introduces

further risks to children, as does the alarming increase in violence against humanitarian aid workers working in complex emergencies of recent years.

A framework for child rights in complex emergencies

The Convention provides a strong legislative framework for realizing child rights in humanitarian crises, particularly articles 38 and 39, and the Optional Protocol on the Involvement of Children in Armed Conflict. Other international norms for protecting children in emergencies have also been strengthened considerably, with a number of UN Security Council resolutions, notably resolutions 1612 and 1820, aimed at ending the abuse of children and civilians in the context of war. The International Criminal Court has launched procedures to investigate and try those alleged to have committed genocide, crimes against humanity and war crimes; the first such case heard by the court concerned the recruitment of child soldiers.

A set of core commitments to child rights in complex emergencies and post-conflict situations has emerged to restore access for women and children to adequate nutrition, disease prevention and control, clean water and decent sanitation as soon as possible. Recent examples of such humanitarian action involving UNICEF in 2008 include a measles campaign reaching children in Myanmar after Cyclone Nargis damaged most of the country's health facilities, and provision of safe drinking water and gender-sensitive toilets for 320,000 children in 500 schools in Afghanistan, along with training in hygiene, sanitation and health for 2,500 teachers.

Inspired by the Convention and its Optional Protocols, child protection has become a priority in emergencies. Humanitarian action now includes establishing child-friendly spaces,

mobilizing communities for child protection, integrating child protection into disaster preparedness, and advocacy and communication. Ensuring that national disaster preparedness plans include child protection has become a priority in certain countries prone to natural disasters, such as Nepal. In the Democratic Republic of the Congo, more than 18,000 survivors of sexual violence – a third of them children – have benefited from medical and psychosocial care, legal counselling and socioeconomic reintegration programmes.

Restoring access to education in emergencies has become an increasingly important component of humanitarian action over the past decade. Enabling children to return to school in communities devastated by violence, war or natural disasters helps reestablish normal routines and gives them a place to learn and play. An even greater challenge is rebuilding education systems in the wake of disaster or conflict and in countries with generally low capacity. In Somalia, which is struggling to re-establish a functioning government after a long period of collapse, 190,300 of the country's estimated 534,000 schoolchildren, including more than 140,000 children in emergency-affected locations, have benefited from renewed distribution of school supplies.

Post-crisis recovery presents an opportunity for societies to build more equitable public institutions to realize the rights of marginalized groups. The international community is now accelerating the development of tools and approaches that address not only the immediate crisis response, but also recovery and preparation for new emergencies. These efforts provide an opportunity to ensure that child rights are secured as early as possible.

See References, pages 90–92.

© UNICEF/NYHQ2004-0392/Antonio Fiorente

Innovative, integrated and collaborative approaches, including children as key partners, are required to fulfil the objectives of the Convention and other international compacts on child rights. *Children aged 9–18 participate in the Fifth Ethiopian Teenagers' Forum at the United Nations Economic Commission for Africa in Addis Ababa, Ethiopia.*

aspects of the Convention for the very first time. With sound leadership, collaboration, advocacy and creativity, the uncertain outlook for the world's economy and environment can also become an opportunity for governments and other stakeholders to renew their commitment to the principles and articles of the Convention, work together to consolidate the gains in child rights and development outcomes achieved over the past two decades, and forge a supportive environment that will advance and safeguard child rights come what may.

Turning crisis into opportunity

For the past 20 years, the international community has continued to set bold objectives to fulfil the rights of children, not least in the shape of the Millennium Development Goals. Efforts to achieve these targets have contributed to important gains in survival, health and education on every continent and in every region. But it has been evident to those working in the field of human development and child rights that greater progress towards these ambitious targets could have been attained had they been made an urgent priority.

The profound financial and economic crisis now engulfing the world may, if nothing else, have opened a debate on global social and economic priorities. With climate change already a reality and population trends set to markedly increase the number of children in the least developed countries, the old way of operating is no longer applicable. In these circumstances, the world has a unique opportunity to reconstruct itself – and to dedicate itself afresh to nurturing not only the physical environment but also its most vulnerable human inhabitants.

The Convention on the Rights of the Child must have a central role in this realignment of priorities. It is well established that investments in children pay enormous dividends, not just in human terms but also in economic terms.[5] Realizing the promise of the Convention in full will certainly involve social transformation. In an era when social transformation may well be a matter of economic expediency and perhaps even human survival, the vision of the Convention can be a lodestar guiding the actions of governments, organizations and individuals towards a more equitable and prosperous future. Perhaps most important, realizing child rights will ensure that all children have the opportunity to attain their full potential, free from violence, abuse, exploitation and neglect, in families, communities and societies that facilitate their survival and development, protection and participation. To paraphrase the words of the 1924 Geneva Declaration of the Rights of the Child, if we truly believe that the world owes its the children the best it has to give, we can do no less.

Climate change and child rights

The Convention on the Rights of the Child envisions a world in which children have the right to survive and grow in a healthy physical environment. Yet child rights, and children themselves, are rarely included in international and national discussions on climate change and how to respond to it.

Children are particularly vulnerable to the impact of climate change for several reasons. First, their stage of physiological and cognitive development and innate curiosity leave them at a heightened risk of exposure to environmental hazards and the potential to be harmed by them. Children are, for instance, more susceptible than adults to the effects of intense ultraviolet radiation, inadequate shelter and indoor air pollution from biomass fuel.

Second, many of the main killers of young children – undernutrition (which contributes to more than one third of all under-five deaths), acute respiratory infections, diarrhoea, malaria and other vector-borne diseases – are known to be highly sensitive to climatic conditions.

Third, there is increasing evidence that the world's least developed countries are likely to bear the brunt of climate change. These countries have large child populations. In 2008, under-18s accounted for 47 per cent of the population in the world's 49 least developed countries, compared with 21 per cent in the industrialized countries. Many developing countries suffer from poor physical infrastructure and lack systems to cope with such climatic events as drought and flooding.

Fourth, the growing correlation between civil strife and climate change is an area of particular concern for child rights. A 2007 study estimated that 46 countries, with a total population of 2.7 billion people, may face a higher risk of violent conflict as climate change intersects with social, economic and political stresses. For children, this has consequences of psychosocial trauma, recruitment into armed forces, displacement and forced migration, which may in turn lead to family separation and exposure to trafficking and exploitation.

Last, the evidence strongly suggests that climate change will make achieving the Millennium Development Goals even more difficult. The Stern Review, a comprehensive study on the economic impact of climate change commissioned by the Government of the United Kingdom in 2006, has estimated that climate change could increase under-five deaths in South Asia and sub-Saharan Africa by 40,000–160,000 annually, by reducing economic output in these regions.

The potential loss of livelihood for millions of families could mean that more children will be needed to support household income, making it more difficult for them, especially girls, to attend school. The increasing scarcity of water and other natural resources will place an even greater burden on girls and women, who undertake most of the household fuel and water collection. And the cost of mitigating climate change may leave less money for social spending on health, education and other social protection programmes.

Children as protagonists in the response to climate change

Integrated, collaborative approaches, with children as key partners, are required to face the complex challenges that climate change poses to child rights. Intersectoral collaboration in the areas of health, education, nutrition and public works and with those agencies and organizations entrusted with the care and protection of children, women, young people and families, will be essential. Gender awareness is also required to create opportunity, reduce vulnerability and empower all citizens. Community partnerships will also be central to mitigation and adaptation strategies. Empowering villages, towns and neighbourhoods to cope with threats will entail greater investment in traditional areas of child development, such as nutrition, health care, education, and water, sanitation and hygiene. It will also encompass innovative interventions to promote renewable energy sources, such as solar and wind, for cooking, heating and water collection; to enhance the availability and quality of environmental education in schools and communities; to support groups whose livelihoods may be threatened; and to improve disaster-preparedness for storms, floods and droughts.

Across the developing world, initiatives have already emerged to address these challenges. In Sierra Leone, for example, 15,000 young people are participating in a volunteer programme that trains them to better run their farms and plots, organize micro-enterprises and share good practices. In Morocco, a World Bank-assisted project aimed at reducing the burden of water collection on girls has succeeded in raising their net primary school attendance by 20 per cent. In Tajikistan, children are helping to test water quality, using simple, inexpensive testing equipment. These examples show how undertaking efforts with children at the centre can create a better natural environment and at the same time help children and young people realize their rights.

Adapting to climate change can provide an opportunity for countries and communities to revitalize their commitments to children. Steps must now be taken to mitigate the effects of climate change and strengthen mechanisms of preparedness and adaptation. The cost of inaction will be high; left unattended, climate change threatens reversals in child survival and development in the 21st century.

See References, pages 90–92.

Child rights in Mexico

Mexico ratified the Convention on 21 September 1990, and successive national governments have worked to support children's rights. Despite a major financial crisis during the mid-1990s, the country has made steady progress in child survival, health care and education. According to the latest international estimates, the under-five mortality rate has been reduced by one third since 1990, net primary school enrolment and routine immunization are above 97 per cent, and 95 per cent of Mexicans have access to improved sources of water.

Mexico has also been a strong advocate for child rights beyond its borders. It was one of the six countries that convened the World Summit for Children in 1990, and it has subsequently helped organize events to monitor States' progress towards meeting their commitments to children. Mexico promoted the formulation and approval of regional guidelines for the protection of unaccompanied migrant children in the Regional Conference on Migration covering North and Central America and the Dominican Republic. The Government has also provided leadership in chairing the UN Security Council Working Group on Children and Armed Conflict.

Linking child protection to health care and other social benefits

Within the country, multi-sectoral programmes involving a broad range of stakeholders are having a positive impact throughout Mexican society. For example, the internationally acclaimed Oportunidades programme, which began in 1997 under the name Progresa, addresses overlapping issues of poverty, ill health, child labour, and school non-attendance and dropout. Oportunidades delivers cash transfers to women on condition that their children attend periodic health checks and go to school. By 2008, it had reached 5 million families in all 31

Mexican states and the Federal District, with around one fifth of the recipient families living in the impoverished southern states of Chiapas and Veracruz.

Mexico has also been engaged in innovative health programmes. During the past 30 years, the country has used the "diagonal approach to health care" to implement and expand successful initiatives to combat diarrhoeal diseases, vaccine-preventable diseases and micronutrient deficiencies. A comprehensive programme of primary health care for mothers, newborns and children – Arranque Parejo en la Vida (Equal Start in Life) – was introduced in 2001 and has reached a high level of national coverage. With the addition of Seguro Popular de Salud, a public health insurance initiative, maternal and child health became entitlements. In 2007, another insurance initiative targeted specifically at newborns – Seguro Médico para una Nueva Generación – was introduced. And in 2009, universal and free health care during pregnancy, childbirth and the post-partum period was launched as part of a national strategy to further reduce maternal mortality.

A diverse country with a federal structure, Mexico continues to be challenged by the complexity of establishing integrated child protection policies and systems. Among these challenges are addressing violence against women and children, sexual exploitation and child labour. The Government of Mexico has taken important steps to regularly collect and disseminate disaggregated data on child labour, adding a module on the issue to the national household employment survey. The 2007 survey revealed that 3.6 million children aged 5 to 17 years old – 12.5 per cent of the age cohort – were engaged in child labour, including 1.1 million children under 14, the legal minimum age of employment. Nearly 42 per cent of working children do not attend school.

Complex challenges across the country's states

Mexico's southern region presents some of the greatest child rights challenges. Home to the majority of the country's indigenous communities – more than 60 ethnic and linguistic groups – it accounts for most of the 20 per cent of Mexicans who live in absolute poverty. Violence perpetrated by organized criminal elements has added to the dangers already posed by ongoing civil conflict here, especially disputes over land rights. As each indigenous community has its own pressing issues, applying human rights legislation uniformly remains a complex task, which the Committee on the Rights of the Child has recognized in its responses to the periodic reports submitted by Mexico since 1990.

Mexico is advancing in its efforts to bring state legislation on child rights into line with national and international law. Its third periodic report to the Committee pointed to the progress individual states are making in ensuring child health, improving domestic and family law, and strengthening child protection.

Hard hit by the global economic crisis, and with violence an urgent concern, Mexico faces a triple task: addressing the disparities that deny children in impoverished and marginalized communities their rights, strengthening child protection systems at the local and national level, and sustaining the overall gains in provision and protection that have been accomplished through its national and targeted initiatives. Further innovation and commitment to child rights will be required to address these challenges in Latin America's second largest country.

See References, pages 90–92.

Developing the capacities of governments, communities, families and children is critical to the greater understanding and promotion of children's rights. *Boys study using their exercise books at Basti Arian Government Boys Primary School in the village of Basti Arian in Rahim Yar Khan District, Punjab Province, Pakistan.*

An agenda for action

The Convention has several primary characteristics. It is a legal instrument, laying down the obligations and responsibilities of governments. It is a guiding framework, underpinned by core principles and comprehensive provisions. It is an ethical statement. And it has been the basis for an expanded and galvanized movement for children, as well as a human-rights based approach for cooperation. These characteristics carry with them a corresponding agenda for action.

- **Make the best interests of the child the primary test of governance.** Laws, policies, budgets, research and systems of governance must reflect the Convention. Interventions must focus on addressing the realities of children's lives to ensure that their best interests are served.

- **Develop capacities to realize the rights of children.** This ranges from empowering parents with the knowledge and skills they need to care for, guide and protect children, to mobilizing communities and supporting those in positions of power to fulfil child rights.

- **Support social and cultural values that respect the rights of children.** Recognizing children as holders of rights, and accepting corresponding responsibilities at every level – from individual to government – is critical to ensuring the rights of

every child. Fundamental to this challenge is honouring children's right to be heard and have their views respected.

- **Work together to meet the promise of the Convention for all children.** No government, donor or agency can meet the multiple child rights challenges alone. The past two decades have taught us that success is often only possible – and almost always most sustainable – through collaborative, integrated approaches.

Make the best interests of the child the primary test of governance

The first challenge for States parties is to assess the implications for children of a wide range of legislative and administrative actions. The second is to ensure that public budgets, policies and programmes apply the Convention's principles in all of their aspects.

Every aspect of governance can affect child rights. Children are best served when governance is democratic and transparent. Not surprisingly, they are undermined by governance failures, such as corruption, inefficiency and political instability. Whether decisions relate to taxation or trade, diplomacy or debt, there is no such thing as a 'child-neutral' policy, law, budget, programme or plan. Children's access to health care requires adequate attention in fiscal budgets to ensure that essential services are provided at the appropriate time in the continuum of maternal, newborn and child care in sufficient quantities and to a high quality. Their education depends on the effectiveness and competence of local education authorities and on adequate investment in physical, technological and human resources. Their protection from violence and abuse demands a functioning legal system and consistent, courageous application of the rule of law – including provisions aimed at preventing abuses of child rights and ending impunity for perpetrators of child protection violations.

> Integrated, collaborative approaches – with children as partners – will be pivotal to meeting the promise of the Convention.

Making the Convention on the Rights of the Child a primary test of governance means that the decisions and actions of governments at all levels must be considered, monitored and evaluated for their implications for child rights. At the national level, budget decisions should take into account their effect on child rights – in particular, on services that are essential for meeting children's rights to survival and development, protection and participation.

In development cooperation, donors and recipient countries must consider how their assistance works for children. In districts and communities, local administrations must ensure that development initiatives are inclusive and participatory, and that the views of women and children are heard, respected and reflected in laws, practices, policies and programmes.

Using the aims of Millennium Declaration and the targets of the Millennium Development Goals as the combined framework for results is a useful way to monitor several key aspects of child rights. The Declaration sets the frame for prioritizing peace and security, stability, and improved development outcomes for children and women.

A further challenge is to embed the Convention into international, national and sub-national legislative systems in both word and deed. It is often noted that laws mean little without enforcement, although having a law in place, even if enforcement is inadequate, is generally preferable to having none. Enforcement implies that law enforcement and judicial systems are able to implement legislation and are held accountable for their failures to act. It also demands adequate budgets to make implementation of laws possible. These duties

apply not only to national governments but also to provincial or district administrations.

Incorporating the Convention into legal systems may entail the establishment, within government, of permanent structures with the overall responsibility of promoting child rights and overseeing coordination between the various sectors and levels of public administration and between government and other stakeholders, including children. The promotion of independent human rights officials, such as child ombudspersons, can also strengthen monitoring of child rights within countries and communities. Greater knowledge and understanding of the situation of children, based on evidence derived from data, research and evaluation, are also critical components for monitoring effective implementation of the Convention.

The principle of universality is critical to making public policies and programmes work for children. The rights of the Convention apply equally to all children, and governance should be judged not by how well some children are served, but rather by how all children are served, including the most disadvantaged. That more than 4 out of 5 of the world's children live in countries where the gap between rich and poor is widening testifies to the fact that realizing child rights is, in large part, a question of equity and social justice.

Develop capacities to realize child rights

The ambition of the Convention is a world where all children enjoy all of their rights; where their survival, development, protection and participation are guaranteed by stakeholders committed to their care and protection as their highest priorities. To achieve such a world will require contributions from every person and institution. All will need to develop their capacity to understand, respond to and promote child rights.

Governments must develop the capacity to make decisions that promote and protect child rights. They must acquire the experience, expertise and knowledge that allow them to build upon the lessons learned by others. Local levels of government, where capacity is often most limited, are not exempt from this obligation.

Professionals in fields as diverse as education, health, urban planning, security services, child protection, civil society organizations and the media should be encouraged and trained to be aware of child rights and of their own responsibilities to act in accordance with those rights. Furthermore, families need the capacity to provide the best possible care

Child rights in Mozambique

In 1992, when the signing of a peace agreement brought an end to 15 years of bitter civil strife, Mozambique ranked as the poorest country in the world. Since then, political stability and democratic governance have paved the way for sustained socio-economic development, and Mozambique is now recognized as an example of post-war reconstruction and economic recovery in Africa. The country held its first democratic elections in 1994, the same year it endorsed the Convention; its third peaceful national elections took place a decade later.

The economy has grown rapidly over the past decade, with gross domestic product for 2008 expected to exceed 6 per cent. The national poverty rate, an estimated 69 per cent in 1997, measured 54 per cent in 2003, the latest year for which comprehensive data are available. Progress in political and economic stability has been accompanied by improved human and social development. The country's under-five mortality rate dropped from 201 deaths per 1,000 live births in 1990 to 168 per 1,000 in 2007. Net primary school attendance rose to 99 per cent in 2008. Despite these advances, Mozambique remains impoverished – 75 per cent of its population lived on less than US$1.25 per day in 2005 – and continues to face such obstacles as recurrent natural disasters and the AIDS epidemic; an estimated 1 in every 7 people aged 15–49 were HIV-positive in 2007.

Creating a protective legal framework for children

During the past two decades, Mozambique has shown a steady commitment to harmonizing national legislation with regional and international human rights instruments. Besides ratifying the Convention, on 26 May 1994, and its two Optional Protocols, the country has also ratified CEDAW, the African Charters on Human and People's Rights (and its protocol on women's rights) and the African charters on the Rights and Welfare of the Child. The national constitution adopted in 2004 places particular emphasis on child rights, setting a new legal and policy framework for children. Under the constitution, all actions concerning children, whether by public bodies or private institutions, must take the 'best interests of the child' into account.

A comprehensive legal reform to update national legislation and bring it into line with the Convention and other human rights treaties has already resulted in major changes, such as an expansion of the period of free birth registration from 30 days to 120 days after a child is born, and adoption of a Family Law that articulates new legal standards for parental responsibilities, guardianship, adoption and inheritance rights, and raises the age of marriage from 16 to 18 years. The Children's Act, adopted in 2008, effectively translates the Convention's articles into national child rights legislation and outlines the responsibilities of all stakeholders in realizing these rights. The 2006–2010 National Action Plan for Children aims to develop and coordinate activities by key stakeholders; its objectives and targets are based on the recommendations of the 2001 African Forum on Children and the 2002 UN Special Session on Children. The Multisectoral Plan for Orphaned and Vulnerable Children addresses the specific needs of this growing population; the number of orphans was estimated at 1.5 million in 2008, of which about 510,000 were orphaned by AIDS.

From legislation and plans to action and results

The main challenge now facing the Government is to translate new legislation into effective programmes. Advances are already apparent in a number of areas. In 2009, the Council of Ministers approved the creation of a National Child Council, an independent body entrusted with coordinating implementation of child rights. Furthermore, special children's court divisions have been established in six provinces to attend to child justice issues. Since 2006, a national birth registration campaign has helped register 4.4 million children; the campaign will continue until 2011, aiming to achieve universal registration by that deadline.

Challenges for realizing children's rights

Poverty and disparities are perhaps the biggest challenges to the realization of child rights in Mozambique. Fighting poverty has been at the top of the Government's agenda during recent years. To be successful, however, scarce budget resources must be allocated equitably to sectors that contribute to children's well-being and development – especially education, health care, water, sanitation and social protection. Within sectors, the equitable allocation of resources across provinces and programmes is also crucial to reducing disparities.

Scaling up basic services and social programmes for children is pivotal to reducing the incidence of child poverty and securing children's rights. The concerted efforts of government, donors, civil society, the media, the corporate sector, families and communities will be necessary to ensure that consistent action is taken to meet the promise of the Convention for all Mozambique's 11 million children.

See References, pages 90–92.

for their children, which entails their having access to food, medical care, housing, schools and clinics – as well as to high-quality and affordable information. As the preamble to the Convention makes abundantly clear, fulfilling the rights of children also demands that families receive the assistance and protection they need to enable them to meet their responsibilities.

Children themselves, of course, must also participate in social progress. As the holders of the rights stipulated in the Convention, it is imperative that children know and understand their rights and are empowered to claim them. The Convention should be taught in schools, so that children can be advocates for themselves. Children also have responsibilities to other children under the Convention: Learning about their own rights entails recognizing the rights of others.

Support social and cultural values that respect child rights

The Convention asserts a set of standards for the care, development and protection of children to which the world's governments have committed themselves. These standards are underpinned by the conviction that all children, regardless of where they were born and in what circumstances, have equal rights; that children should come first in public policies and programmes, in times of conflict and emergency as well as in times of peace and stability; and that their rights imply responsibilities for all people who can contribute to their fulfilment.

These values, however, are not always upheld throughout society and can be undermined by long-established cultural traditions or assumptions. Social and cultural practices such as child marriage, female genital mutilation/cutting and discrimination – whether on the basis of gender, ethnicity, disability, religion or class – all currently play their part in undermining child rights. These are grave problems that demand our urgent attention. Denying children their rights on the basis of gender, ethnicity, disability or any other discriminating factor is unacceptable. When children's rights are routinely disregarded, when the global neglect of child rights continues to allow millions of children to be deprived of access to essential services, then it is the duty of all to take responsibility and contribute to the solution.

In this sense the need for a change in values links back to the history of the Convention and the campaigns for child rights that preceded it. Those campaigners who were outraged by the treatment of children in 19th-century factories or by their

To make the vision of the Convention a reality for every child, it must become a guiding document for every human being. *An 18-year-old boy advocates against the sexual exploitation and abuse of children, and participates in several child rights groups in his community in Lusaka, Zambia.*

© UNICEF/NYHQ2006-1268/Francois d'Elbee

victimization in times of world war would be no less outraged by the high incidence of child labour in the world today or the continued use of child soldiers. Children around the world continue to endure conditions tantamount to slavery. They are trafficked to other countries and exploited as forced labourers or prostitutes. They are brutalized and victimized as participants in wars to an extent that allows today's world no self-satisfied sense of moral superiority over yesterday's. They are often not afforded dignity and worth when they come into conflict with the law.

As we approach the end of this first decade of the 21st century, nearly 9 million children still die each year before their fifth birthday, more than 140 million under-fives suffer from undernutrition, roughly 100 million primary-school-age children do not receive an education, and an estimated 150 million children age 5–14 years are engaged in child labour. The experience of each one of these children, along with others excluded from essential services or suffering protection violations and discrimination, is a testament to the need for a profound change of values. Anyone – whether a politician, administrator, media analyst or simply an opinionated layperson – who accepts this neglect as the inevitable way of the world is failing in his or her responsibility to the world's children.

Child rights in Serbia

Serbia has undergone a profound transformation since the cold war ended 20 years ago, and despite enduring more than a decade of political turmoil, it is making steady progress in improving outcomes for children in primary health care and education.

At just 8 deaths per 1,000 live births in 2007, its under-five mortality rate is one of the lowest in the CEE/CIS region. Routine immunization, measured by the percentage of infants receiving three doses of diphtheria, pertussis and tetanus toxoid vaccine, stood at 94 per cent. Almost 99 per cent of its population has access to improved drinking-water facilities, and 92 per cent have access to adequate sanitation. Education is readily accessible, with net primary school attendance at 98 per cent in 2000–2007, and net secondary school attendance at 90 per cent for both girls and boys.

Children still vulnerable to social exclusion and lack of parental care

Despite these gains, poverty, disparities and high levels of social exclusion among vulnerable groups remain pressing concerns. Children living in rural areas and the less developed parts of the country are at risk of being excluded from essential services and protection not only because of income but also because of sociocultural poverty and discrimination. More than 155,000 children are living below the national poverty line, with a similar number at risk of falling into poverty. Among the Roma, one of the country's largest ethnic minorities, under-five mortality is more than three times higher than the national average.

In addition, in its concluding observations on child rights in Serbia in 2008, the Committee on the Rights of the Child expressed concern regarding the large number of Serbian children with disabilities who remain institutionalized. Research shows that children living in institutions are particularly vulnerable to neglect, abuse and violence and that these risks may increase for those who also live with disability. A recent study of the situation in Serbia by Mental Disabilities Rights International found that children with disabilities in residential care are segregated from society and forced to live in institutions throughout their lives. They often lack skilled caregivers and are not integrated into the education system.

Establishing a framework of protection

The Government of Serbia has developed national strategies and action plans to reduce the risk of social exclusion. The overall framework for enhancing child protection is based on the Convention on the Rights of the Child and incorporates key strategic documents, including Serbia's Poverty Reduction Strategy Paper and its National Plan of Action for Children. The plan of action sets targets to reduce child poverty, provide quality education, protect the rights of children deprived of parental care and establish a comprehensive system of protection from violence, abuse, exploitation and neglect.

The Government of Serbia is also implementing strategies to care for and protect vulnerable children. The 2007–2015 Strategy for Improving the Position of Persons with Disabilities includes programmes aimed at expanding access to essential services, protection and participation for children living with disability, while the framework of the 2005–2015 Roma Decade focuses on social protection for Roma children. A juvenile justice code adopted in 2006 outlines provisions to protect children who are in conflict with the law.

Galvanizing reform

For the past five years, the Government of Serbia has taken steps towards reforming its social protection system through its Social Welfare Development Strategy. Deinstitutionalization is one of the main goals of the reform process, which requires setting up a network of community-based social services, with corresponding standards to ensure quality of care. Positive trends have been observed since implementation of the plan; for example, the number of children without parental care in residential institutions has been reduced, with a corresponding increase in foster placements. The deinstitutionalization of children with disabilities, however, is still nascent.

To galvanize the reform process, the Ministry of Labour and Social Policy recently signed a memorandum of understanding with UNICEF. The four main strategic goals include transformation of all residential institutions for children; new standards of accountability for professionals for protection of child rights; inter-municipal, decentralized plans for community-based support services for families and children; and the establishment of specialized foster care for children with disabilities.

The Government of Serbia is making determined strides to promote and protect the rights of the child, despite emerging pressures from the global economic crisis. In addition to the reform of its social protection system, it is seeking to build a national child protection system that connects legislation, budgets, policies, programmes and research. A major challenge lies in implementing this inter-sectoral approach to ensure access to the continuum of services, protection and participation for all children, particularly those who are currently excluded due to discrimination, neglect and poverty.

See References, pages 90–92.

Child rights in Sweden

Whenever measures of social progress or human development are published, it is usual to find Sweden – along with its Nordic neighbours, Denmark, Finland, Iceland and Norway – close to the top. All five nations rank among the top 15 in the United Nations Development Programme's *Human Development Index 2008* (based on 2006 data), with Sweden in seventh place. The country ranked first in the Economist Intelligence Unit's *Democracy Index 2008* and third best in Transparency International's *Corruption Perceptions Index* for the same year.

Sweden's high level of social development reflects a democratic and stable political system and high standards of living. In 2006, GDP per capita, in purchasing power parity terms, stood at US$34,000. A sound health-care system has reduced mortality rates at all levels to low rates. The latest UN inter-agency estimates show the under-five mortality rate for 2007 at 3 deaths per 1,000 live births and the lifetime risk of maternal mortality at 1 in 17,400. Education is universal at both the primary and secondary levels.

A strong supporter of the Convention while it was being drafted, Sweden was one of the first countries to ratify the treaty, on 29 June 1990, and has also ratified its two Optional Protocols. The country's focus on meeting children's needs and fulfilling their rights predates the Convention, however. Since the early 1970s, it has been actively committed to providing children with necessary care and support, especially in health and education, through innovative, well-resourced government policies and programmes. Abroad, the Swedish International Development Cooperation Agency has a long history of engagement and investment in child rights across the developing world.

Among the 30 member states of the Organisation for Economic Co-operation and Development, Sweden spends the most on the preschool child. And it was the only country of 25 with comparable data to achieve all 10 benchmarks for early childhood care and education in a 2008 study by UNICEF's Innocenti Research Centre.

One example of this attentiveness to child rights is the Swedish Government's Early Childhood Education and Care programme, which has been given high priority during recent decades and forms a cornerstone of family policy. Research has consistently shown the benefits of early childhood care, which is strongly advocated in General Comment No. 7 to the Convention. Pedagogic activities and stimulation form a strong foundation for development and learning and contribute to better educational outcomes in primary, secondary and tertiary levels – which in turn support higher average earnings and better living standards. To encourage such early childhood development, parents in Sweden have a right to take more than two years of temporary leave to care for infants and young children. In addition, the Early Childhood Education and Care programme helps working parents balance parenthood with work and studies.

This programme and other child-friendly initiatives are the responsibility of the Ministry of Health and Social Affairs, one of whose functions is to ensure that child rights are considered in all areas of government policy and public affairs affecting children and young people. To this end, in 1999 the Swedish Parliament adopted a national strategy for the implementation of the Convention. The objective of this approach is to foster respect for the principles that underpin the Convention; provide essential services, protection

and opportunities for development; protect children against harm and neglect; and encourage their participation in the community and throughout society.

To further protect child rights, the Government of Sweden has appointed a children's ombudsperson to represent the interests of children and young people and monitor compliance with the Convention at all levels of society. Each year, the ombudsperson submits a report to the Government on the situation of the country's children and young people, highlighting the opportunities and obstacles encountered in fulfilling their rights.

This firm framework for child rights is not without its challenges. Like other industrialized countries, Sweden is experiencing an increase in the number of children and young people who suffer from psychological distress and obesity. In its concluding observations to the country's fourth periodic report, presented in 2007, the Committee on the Rights of the Child expressed concern at the broad disparities among municipalities, counties and regions in the implementation of the Convention, and recommended that the Government strengthen measures to guarantee equal access and availability of services for all children, regardless of where they live. Sweden has also experienced significant immigration during recent decades and faces the task of ensuring that the rights of immigrant children are met. Strengthening mechanisms to address the rights of children belonging to vulnerable groups – including unaccompanied, refugee and asylum-seeking children – is a relatively new challenge, one that Sweden is well placed to confront, given its legacy of respect for and commitment to child rights.

See References, pages 90–92.

Supporting social and cultural values that promote the rights of children is central to protecting them from violence, abuse, exploitation, discrimination and neglect. *A boy plays with his baby sister in Aragam Bay Village in the eastern Ampara District, Sri Lanka.*

Work together to meet the promise of the Convention

The Convention speaks to the ways in which societies must orient themselves differently, and to the values by which they must be judged. By committing States parties to place the best interests of children at the heart of their actions, it has galvanized progress in the areas of legal reform, institutional reform, provision of essential services, awareness raising and political commitment to children.

By providing a focal point for action and enshrining rights in law, the Convention has inspired individuals and organizations to work together. As a result, it has become abundantly clear that broad partnerships are vital to the realization of children's rights, and that children can be the most essential partners in this process. Collaborations in health, education, protection and participation have expanded and strengthened in recent years; they offer the promise of faster progress on child rights and towards internationally agreed development goals for children. But greater collaboration is required between national and international stakeholders, and between larger agents and smaller ones such as district and community entities and local non-government organizations.

The Convention on the Rights of the Child was long fought for and hard won. It is a precious document that charts our course to a world in which children's rights are fulfilled and in which all aspects of human well-being immeasurably improve as a result. Building on the solid foundation of the Universal Declaration of Human Rights and other seminal instruments, the Convention has enriched our understanding of human rights by interpreting these rights for children, who are among the most vulnerable of us to economic, security, climatic and epidemiological risks. In this time of crisis and uncertainty, 20 years after the Convention's adoption, we must seize the opportunity to put its principles into practice. The great challenge for the next 20 years will be to unite governmental accountability with social and individual responsibility. To make the vision of the Convention a reality for every child, it must become a guiding document for every human being.

The Convention on the Rights of the Child

The Convention on the Rights of the Child was adopted and opened for signature, ratification and accession by General Assembly resolution 44/25 of 20 November 1989. It entered into force 2 September 1990, in accordance with article 49. It has been ratified by 193 countries.

Preamble

The States Parties to the present Convention,

Considering that, in accordance with the principles proclaimed in the Charter of the United Nations, recognition of the inherent dignity and of the equal and inalienable rights of all members of the human family is the foundation of freedom, justice and peace in the world,

Bearing in mind that the peoples of the United Nations have, in the Charter, reaffirmed their faith in fundamental human rights and in the dignity and worth of the human person and have determined to promote social progress and better standards of life in larger freedom,

Recognizing that the United Nations has, in the Universal Declaration of Human Rights and in the International Covenants on Human Rights, proclaimed and agreed that everyone is entitled to all the rights and freedoms set forth therein, without distinction of any kind, such as race, colour, sex, language, religion, political or other opinion, national or social origin, property, birth or other status,

Recalling that, in the Universal Declaration of Human Rights, the United Nations has proclaimed that childhood is entitled to special care and assistance,

Convinced that the family, as the fundamental group of society and the natural environment for the growth and well-being of all its members and particularly children, should be afforded the necessary protection and assistance so that it can fully assume its responsibilities within the community,

Recognizing that the child, for the full and harmonious development of his or her personality, should grow up in a family environment, in an atmosphere of happiness, love and understanding,

Considering that the child should be fully prepared to live an individual life in society and brought up in the spirit of the ideals proclaimed in the Charter of the United Nations and in particular in the spirit of peace, dignity, tolerance, freedom, equality and solidarity,

Bearing in mind that the need to extend particular care to the child has been stated in the Geneva Declaration of the Rights of the Child of 1924 and in the Declaration of the Rights of the Child adopted by the General Assembly on 20 November 1959 and recognized in the Universal Declaration of Human Rights, in the International Covenant on Civil and Political Rights (in particular in articles 23 and 24), in the International Covenant on Economic, Social and Cultural Rights (in particular in article 10) and in the statutes and relevant instruments of specialized agencies and international organizations concerned with the welfare of children,

Bearing in mind that, as indicated in the Declaration of the Rights of the Child, "the child, by reason of his physical and mental immaturity, needs special safeguards and care, including appropriate legal protection, before as well as after birth",

Recalling the provisions of the Declaration on Social and Legal Principles relating to the Protection and Welfare of Children, with Special Reference to Foster Placement and Adoption Nationally and Internationally; the United Nations Standard Minimum Rules for the Administration of Juvenile Justice (The Beijing Rules); and the Declaration on the Protection of Women and Children in Emergency and Armed Conflict,

Recognizing that, in all countries in the world, there are children living in exceptionally difficult conditions and that such children need special consideration,

Taking due account of the importance of the traditions and cultural values of each people for the protection and harmonious development of the child,

Recognizing the importance of international co-operation for improving the living conditions of children in every country, in particular in the developing countries,

Have agreed as follows:

Part I

Article 1

For the purposes of the present Convention, a child means every human being below the age of eighteen years unless under the law applicable to the child, majority is attained earlier.

Article 2

1. States Parties shall respect and ensure the rights set forth in the present Convention to each child within their jurisdiction without discrimination of any kind, irrespective of the child's or his or her parent's or legal guardian's race, colour, sex, language, religi on, political or other opinion, national, ethnic or social origin, property, disability, birth or other status.

2. States Parties shall take all appropriate measures to ensure that the child is protected against all forms of discrimination or punishment on the basis of the status, activities, expressed opinions, or beliefs of the child's parents, legal guardians, or family members.

Article 3

1. In all actions concerning children, whether undertaken by public or private social welfare institutions, courts of law, administrative authorities or legislative bodies, the best interests of the child shall be a primary consideration.

2. States Parties undertake to ensure the child such protection and care as is necessary for his or her well-being, taking into account the rights and duties of his or her parents, legal guardians, or other individuals legally responsible for him or her, and, to this end, shall take all appropriate legislative and administrative measures.

3. States Parties shall ensure that the institutions, services and facilities responsible for the care or protection of children shall conform with the standards established by competent authorities, particularly in the areas of safety, health, in the number and suitability of their staff, as well as competent supervision.

Article 4

States Parties shall undertake all appropriate legislative, administrative and other measures for the implementation of the rights recognized in the present Convention. With regard to economic, social and cultural rights, States Parties shall undertake such measures to the maximum extent of their available resources and, where needed, within the framework of international co-operation.

Article 5

States Parties shall respect the responsibilities, rights and duties of parents or, where applicable, the members of the extended family or community as provided for by local custom, legal guardians or other persons legally responsible for the child, to provide, in a manner consistent with the evolving capacities of the child, appropriate direction and guidance in the exercise by the child of the rights recognized in the present Convention.

Article 6

1. States Parties recognize that every child has the inherent right to life.

2. States Parties shall ensure to the maximum extent possible the survival and development of the child.

Article 7

1. The child shall be registered immediately after birth and shall have the right from birth to a name, the right to acquire a nationality and, as far as possible, the right to know and be cared for by his or her parents.

2. States Parties shall ensure the implementation of these rights in accordance with their national law and their obligations under the relevant international instruments in this field, in particular where the child would otherwise be stateless.

Article 8

1. States Parties undertake to respect the right of the child to preserve his or her identity, including nationality, name and family relations as recognized by law without unlawful interference.

2. Where a child is illegally deprived of some or all of the elements of his or her identity, States Parties shall provide appropriate assistance and protection, with a view to re-establishing speedily his or her identity.

Article 9

1. States Parties shall ensure that a child shall not be separated from his or her parents against their will, except when competent authorities subject to judicial review determine, in accordance with applicable law and procedures, that such separation is necessary for the best interests of the child. Such determination may be necessary in a particular case such as one involving abuse or neglect of the child by the parents, or one where the parents are living separately and a decision must be made as to the child's place of residence.

2. In any proceedings pursuant to paragraph 1 of the present article, all interested parties shall be given an opportunity to participate in the proceedings and make their views known.

3. States Parties shall respect the right of the child who is separated from one or both parents to maintain personal relations and direct contact with both parents on a regular basis, except if it is contrary to the child's best interests.

4. Where such separation results from any action initiated by a State Party, such as the detention, imprisonment, exile,

deportation or death (including death arising from any cause while the person is in the custody of the State) of one or both parents or of the child, that State Party shall, upon request, provide the parents, the child or, if appropriate, another member of the family with the essential information concerning the whereabouts of the absent member(s) of the family unless the provision of the information would be detrimental to the well-being of the child. States Parties shall further ensure that the submission of such a request shall of itself entail no adverse consequences for the person(s) concerned.

Article 10

1. In accordance with the obligation of States Parties under article 9, paragraph 1, applications by a child or his or her parents to enter or leave a State Party for the purpose of family reunification shall be dealt with by States Parties in a positive, humane and expeditious manner. States Parties shall further ensure that the submission of such a request shall entail no adverse consequences for the applicants and for the members of their family.

2. A child whose parents reside in different States shall have the right to maintain on a regular basis, save in exceptional circumstances personal relations and direct contacts with both parents. Towards that end and in accordance with the obligation of States Parties under article 9, paragraph 1, States Parties shall respect the right of the child and his or her parents to leave any country, including their own and to enter their own country. The right to leave any country shall be subject only to such restrictions as are prescribed by law and which are necessary to protect the national security, public order (ordre public), public health or morals or the rights and freedoms of others and are consistent with the other rights recognized in the present Convention.

Article 11

1. States Parties shall take measures to combat the illicit transfer and non-return of children abroad.

2. To this end, States Parties shall promote the conclusion of bilateral or multilateral agreements or accession to existing agreements.

Article 12

1. States Parties shall assure to the child who is capable of forming his or her own views the right to express those views freely in all matters affecting the child, the views of the child being given due weight in accordance with the age and maturity of the child.

2. For this purpose, the child shall in particular be provided the opportunity to be heard in any judicial and administrative proceedings affecting the child, either directly, or through a representative or an appropriate body, in a manner consistent with the procedural rules of national law.

Article 13

1. The child shall have the right to freedom of expression; this right shall include freedom to seek, receive and impart information and ideas of all kinds, regardless of frontiers, either orally, in writing or in print, in the form of art, or through any other media of the child's choice.

2. The exercise of this right may be subject to certain restrictions, but these shall only be such as are provided by law and are necessary:
   (a) For respect of the rights or reputations of others; or
   (b) For the protection of national security or of public order (ordre public), or of public health or morals.

Article 14

1. States Parties shall respect the right of the child to freedom of thought, conscience and religion.

2. States Parties shall respect the rights and duties of the parents and, when applicable, legal guardians, to provide direction to the child in the exercise of his or her right in a manner consistent with the evolving capacities of the child.

3. Freedom to manifest one's religion or beliefs may be subject only to such limitations as are prescribed by law and are necessary to protect public safety, order, health or morals, or the fundamental rights and freedoms of others.

Article 15

1. States Parties recognize the rights of the child to freedom of association and to freedom of peaceful assembly.

2. No restrictions may be placed on the exercise of these rights other than those imposed in conformity with the law and which are necessary in a democratic society in the interests of national security or public safety, public order (ordre public), the protection of public health or morals or the protection of the rights and freedoms of others.

Article 16

1. No child shall be subjected to arbitrary or unlawful interference with his or her privacy, family, home or correspondence, nor to unlawful attacks on his or her honour and reputation.

2. The child has the right to the protection of the law against such interference or attacks.

Article 17

States Parties recognize the important function performed by the mass media and shall ensure that the child has access to information and material from a diversity of national and international sources, especially those aimed at the promotion of his or her social, spiritual and moral well-being and physical and mental health. To this end, States Parties shall:
   (a) Encourage the mass media to disseminate information and material of social and cultural benefit to the child and in accordance with the spirit of article 29;
   (b) Encourage international co-operation in the production,

exchange and dissemination of such information and material from a diversity of cultural, national and international sources;

(c) Encourage the production and dissemination of children's books;

(d) Encourage the mass media to have particular regard to the linguistic needs of the child who belongs to a minority group or who is indigenous;

(e) Encourage the development of appropriate guidelines for the protection of the child from information and material injurious to his or her well-being, bearing in mind the provisions of articles 13 and 18.

Article 18

1. States Parties shall use their best efforts to ensure recognition of the principle that both parents have common responsibilities for the upbringing and development of the child. Parents or, as the case may be, legal guardians, have the primary responsibility for the upbringing and development of the child. The best interests of the child will be their basic concern.

2. For the purpose of guaranteeing and promoting the rights set forth in the present Convention, States Parties shall render appropriate assistance to parents and legal guardians in the performance of their child-rearing responsibilities and shall ensure the development of institutions, facilities and services for the care of children.

3. States Parties shall take all appropriate measures to ensure that children of working parents have the right to benefit from child-care services and facilities for which they are eligible.

Article 19

1. States Parties shall take all appropriate legislative, administrative, social and educational measures to protect the child from all forms of physical or mental violence, injury or abuse, neglect or negligent treatment, maltreatment or exploitation, including sexual abuse, while in the care of parent(s), legal guardian(s) or any other person who has the care of the child.

2. Such protective measures should, as appropriate, include effective procedures for the establishment of social programmes to provide necessary support for the child and for those who have the care of the child, as well as for other forms of prevention and for identification, reporting, referral, investigation, treatment and follow-up of instances of child maltreatment described heretofore, and, as appropriate, for judicial involvement.

Article 20

1. A child temporarily or permanently deprived of his or her family environment, or in whose own best interests cannot be allowed to remain in that environment, shall be entitled to special protection and assistance provided by the State.

2. States Parties shall in accordance with their national laws ensure alternative care for such a child.

3. Such care could include, *inter alia*, foster placement, *kafalah* of Islamic law, adoption or if necessary placement in suitable institutions for the care of children. When considering solutions, due regard shall be paid to the desirability of continuity in a child's upbringing and to the child's ethnic, religious, cultural and linguistic background.

Article 21

States Parties that recognize and/or permit the system of adoption shall ensure that the best interests of the child shall be the paramount consideration and they shall:

(a) Ensure that the adoption of a child is authorized only by competent authorities who determine, in accordance with applicable law and procedures and on the basis of all pertinent and reliable information, that the adoption is permissible in view of the child's status concerning parents, relatives and legal guardians and that, if required, the persons concerned have given their informed consent to the adoption on the basis of such counselling as may be necessary;

(b) Recognize that inter-country adoption may be considered as an alternative means of child's care, if the child cannot be placed in a foster or an adoptive family or cannot in any suitable manner be cared for in the child's country of origin;

(c) Ensure that the child concerned by inter-country adoption enjoys safeguards and standards equivalent to those existing in the case of national adoption;

(d) Take all appropriate measures to ensure that, in inter-country adoption, the placement does not result in improper financial gain for those involved in it;

(e) Promote, where appropriate, the objectives of the present article by concluding bilateral or multilateral arrangements or agreements and endeavour, within this framework, to ensure that the placement of the child in another country is carried out by competent authorities or organs.

Article 22

1. States Parties shall take appropriate measures to ensure that a child who is seeking refugee status or who is considered a refugee in accordance with applicable international or domestic law and procedures shall, whether unaccompanied or accompanied by his or her parents or by any other person, receive appropriate protection and humanitarian assistance in the enjoyment of applicable rights set forth in the present Convention and in other international human rights or humanitarian instruments to which the said States are Parties.

2. For this purpose, States Parties shall provide, as they consider appropriate, co-operation in any efforts by the United Nations and other competent intergovernmental organizations or

non-governmental organizations co-operating with the United Nations to protect and assist such a child and to trace the parents or other members of the family of any refugee child in order to obtain information necessary for reunification with his or her family. In cases where no parents or other members of the family can be found, the child shall be accorded the same protection as any other child permanently or temporarily deprived of his or her family environment for any reason, as set forth in the present Convention.

Article 23

1. States Parties recognize that a mentally or physically disabled child should enjoy a full and decent life, in conditions which ensure dignity, promote self-reliance and facilitate the child's active participation in the community.

2. States Parties recognize the right of the disabled child to special care and shall encourage and ensure the extension, subject to available resources, to the eligible child and those responsible for his or her care, of assistance for which application is made and which is appropriate to the child's condition and to the circumstances of the parents or others caring for the child.

3. Recognizing the special needs of a disabled child, assistance extended in accordance with paragraph 2 of the present article shall be provided free of charge, whenever possible, taking into account the financial resources of the parents or others caring for the child and shall be designed to ensure that the disabled child has effective access to and receives education, training, health care services, rehabilitation services, preparation for employment and recreation opportunities in a manner conducive to the child's achieving the fullest possible social integration and individual development, including his or her cultural and spiritual development.

4. States Parties shall promote, in the spirit of international cooperation, the exchange of appropriate information in the field of preventive health care and of medical, psychological and functional treatment of disabled children, including dissemination of and access to information concerning methods of rehabilitation, education and vocational services, with the aim of enabling States Parties to improve their capabilities and skills and to widen their experience in these areas. In this regard, particular account shall be taken of the needs of developing countries.

Article 24

1. States Parties recognize the right of the child to the enjoyment of the highest attainable standard of health and to facilities for the treatment of illness and rehabilitation of health. States Parties shall strive to ensure that no child is deprived of his or her right of access to such health care services.

2. States Parties shall pursue full implementation of this right and, in particular, shall take appropriate measures:

(a) To diminish infant and child mortality;

(b) To ensure the provision of necessary medical assistance and health care to all children with emphasis on the development of primary health care;

(c) To combat disease and malnutrition, including within the framework of primary health care, through, *inter alia*, the application of readily available technology and through the provision of adequate nutritious foods and clean drinking-water, taking into consideration the dangers and risks of environmental pollution;

(d) To ensure appropriate pre-natal and post-natal health care for mothers;

(e) To ensure that all segments of society, in particular parents and children, are informed, have access to education and are supported in the use of basic knowledge of child health and nutrition, the advantages of breastfeeding, hygiene and environmental sanitation and the prevention of accidents;

(f) To develop preventive health care, guidance for parents and family planning education and services.

3. States Parties shall take all effective and appropriate measures with a view to abolishing traditional practices prejudicial to the health of children.

4. States Parties undertake to promote and encourage international cooperation with a view to achieving progressively the full realization of the right recognized in the present article. In this regard, particular account shall be taken of the needs of developing countries.

Article 25

States Parties recognize the right of a child who has been placed by the competent authorities for the purposes of care, protection or treatment of his or her physical or mental health, to a periodic review of the treatment provided to the child and all other circumstances relevant to his or her placement.

Article 26

1. States Parties shall recognize for every child the right to benefit from social security, including social insurance and shall take the necessary measures to achieve the full realization of this right in accordance with their national law.

2. The benefits should, where appropriate, be granted, taking into account the resources and the circumstances of the child and persons having responsibility for the maintenance of the child, as well as any other consideration relevant to an application for benefits made by or on behalf of the child.

Article 27

1. States Parties recognize the right of every child to a standard of living adequate for the child's physical, mental, spiritual, moral and social development.

2. The parent(s) or others responsible for the child have the primary responsibility to secure, within their abilities and

financial capacities, the conditions of living necessary for the child's development.

3. States Parties, in accordance with national conditions and within their means, shall take appropriate measures to assist parents and others responsible for the child to implement this right and shall in case of need provide material assistance and support programmes, particularly with regard to nutrition, clothing and housing.

4. States Parties shall take all appropriate measures to secure the recovery of maintenance for the child from the parents or other persons having financial responsibility for the child, both within the State Party and from abroad. In particular, where the person having financial responsibility for the child lives in a State different from that of the child, States Parties shall promote the accession to international agreements or the conclusion of such agreements, as well as the making of other appropriate arrangements.

Article 28

1. States Parties recognize the right of the child to education and with a view to achieving this right progressively and on the basis of equal opportunity, they shall, in particular:
   (a) Make primary education compulsory and available free to all;
   (b) Encourage the development of different forms of secondary education, including general and vocational education, make them available and accessible to every child and take appropriate measures such as the introduction of free education and offering financial assistance in case of need;
   (c) Make higher education accessible to all on the basis of capacity by every appropriate means;
   (d) Make educational and vocational information and guidance available and accessible to all children;
   (e) Take measures to encourage regular attendance at schools and the reduction of drop-out rates.

2. States Parties shall take all appropriate measures to ensure that school discipline is administered in a manner consistent with the child's human dignity and in conformity with the present Convention.

3. States Parties shall promote and encourage international cooperation in matters relating to education, in particular with a view to contributing to the elimination of ignorance and illiteracy throughout the world and facilitating access to scientific and technical knowledge and modern teaching methods. In this regard, particular account shall be taken of the needs of developing countries.

Article 29

1. States Parties agree that the education of the child shall be directed to:
   (a) The development of the child's personality, talents and mental and physical abilities to their fullest potential;
   (b) The development of respect for human rights and fundamental freedoms, and for the principles enshrined in the Charter of the United Nations;
   (c) The development of respect for the child's parents, his or her own cultural identity, language and values, for the national values of the country in which the child is living, the country from which he or she may originate, and for civilizations different from his or her own;
   (d) The preparation of the child for responsible life in a free society, in the spirit of understanding, peace, tolerance, equality of sexes, and friendship among all peoples, ethnic, national and religious groups and persons of indigenous origin;
   (e) The development of respect for the natural environment.

2. No part of the present article or article 28 shall be construed so as to interfere with the liberty of individuals and bodies to establish and direct educational institutions, subject always to the observance of the principle set forth in paragraph 1 of the present article and to the requirements that the education given in such institutions shall conform to such minimum standards as may be laid down by the State.

Article 30

In those States in which ethnic, religious or linguistic minorities or persons of indigenous origin exist, a child belonging to such a minority or who is indigenous shall not be denied the right, in community with other members of his or her group, to enjoy his or her own culture, to profess and practise his or her own religion, or to use his or her own language.

Article 31

1. States Parties recognize the right of the child to rest and leisure, to engage in play and recreational activities appropriate to the age of the child and to participate freely in cultural life and the arts.

2. States Parties shall respect and promote the right of the child to participate fully in cultural and artistic life and shall encourage the provision of appropriate and equal opportunities for cultural, artistic, recreational and leisure activity.

Article 32

1. States Parties recognize the right of the child to be protected from economic exploitation and from performing any work that is likely to be hazardous or to interfere with the child's education, or to be harmful to the child's health or physical, mental, spiritual, moral or social development.

2. States Parties shall take legislative, administrative, social and educational measures to ensure the implementation of the present article. To this end and having regard to the relevant provisions of other international instruments, States Parties shall in particular:
   (a) Provide for a minimum age or minimum ages for admission to employment;
   (b) Provide for appropriate regulation of the hours and conditions of employment;

(c) Provide for appropriate penalties or other sanctions to ensure the effective enforcement of the present article.

Article 33

States Parties shall take all appropriate measures, including legislative, administrative, social and educational measures, to protect children from the illicit use of narcotic drugs and psychotropic substances as defined in the relevant international treaties and to prevent the use of children in the illicit production and trafficking of such substances.

Article 34

States Parties undertake to protect the child from all forms of sexual exploitation and sexual abuse. For these purposes, States Parties shall in particular take all appropriate national, bilateral and multilateral measures to prevent:

(a) The inducement or coercion of a child to engage in any unlawful sexual activity;

(b) The exploitative use of children in prostitution or other unlawful sexual practices;

(c) The exploitative use of children in pornographic performances and materials.

Article 35

States Parties shall take all appropriate national, bilateral and multilateral measures to prevent the abduction of, the sale of or traffic in children for any purpose or in any form.

Article 36

States Parties shall protect the child against all other forms of exploitation prejudicial to any aspects of the child's welfare.

Article 37

States Parties shall ensure that:

(a) No child shall be subjected to torture or other cruel, inhuman or degrading treatment or punishment. Neither capital punishment nor life imprisonment without possibility of release shall be imposed for offences committed by persons below eighteen years of age;

(b) No child shall be deprived of his or her liberty unlawfully or arbitrarily. The arrest, detention or imprisonment of a child shall be in conformity with the law and shall be used only as a measure of last resort and for the shortest appropriate period of time;

(c) Every child deprived of liberty shall be treated with humanity and respect for the inherent dignity of the human person and in a manner which takes into account the needs of persons of his or her age. In particular, every child deprived of liberty shall be separated from adults unless it is considered in the child's best interest not to do so and shall have the right to maintain contact with his or her family through correspondence and visits, save in exceptional circumstances;

(d) Every child deprived of his or her liberty shall have the right to prompt access to legal and other appropriate assistance, as well as the right to challenge the legality of the deprivation of his or her liberty before a court or other competent, independent and impartial authority and to a prompt decision on any such action.

Article 38

1. States Parties undertake to respect and to ensure respect for rules of international humanitarian law applicable to them in armed conflicts which are relevant to the child.

2. States Parties shall take all feasible measures to ensure that persons who have not attained the age of fifteen years do not take a direct part in hostilities.

3. States Parties shall refrain from recruiting any person who has not attained the age of fifteen years into their armed forces. In recruiting among those persons who have attained the age of fifteen years but who have not attained the age of eighteen years, States Parties shall endeavour to give priority to those who are oldest.

4. In accordance with their obligations under international humanitarian law to protect the civilian population in armed conflicts, States Parties shall take all feasible measures to ensure protection and care of children who are affected by an armed conflict.

Article 39

States Parties shall take all appropriate measures to promote physical and psychological recovery and social reintegration of a child victim of: any form of neglect, exploitation, or abuse; torture or any other form of cruel, inhuman or degrading treatment or punishment; or armed conflicts. Such recovery and reintegration shall take place in an environment which fosters the health, self-respect and dignity of the child.

Article 40

1. States Parties recognize the right of every child alleged as, accused of, or recognized as having infringed the penal law to be treated in a manner consistent with the promotion of the child's sense of dignity and worth, which reinforces the child's respect for the human rights and fundamental freedoms of others and which takes into account the child's age and the desirability of promoting the child's reintegration and the child's assuming a constructive role in society.

2. To this end and having regard to the relevant provisions of international instruments, States Parties shall, in particular, ensure that:

(a) No child shall be alleged as, be accused of, or recognized as having infringed the penal law by reason of acts or omissions that were not prohibited by national or international law at the time they were committed;

(b) Every child alleged as or accused of having infringed the penal law has at least the following guarantees:

(i) To be presumed innocent until proven guilty according to law;

(ii) To be informed promptly and directly of the charges against him or her, and, if appropriate, through his or her parents or legal guardians and to have legal or other appropriate assistance in the preparation and presentation of his or her defence;

(iii) To have the matter determined without delay by a competent, independent and impartial authority or judicial body in a fair hearing according to law, in the presence of legal or other appropriate assistance and, unless it is considered not to be in the best interest of the child, in particular, taking into account his or her age or situation, his or her parents or legal guardians;

(iv) Not to be compelled to give testimony or to confess guilt; to examine or have examined adverse witnesses and to obtain the participation and examination of witnesses on his or her behalf under conditions of equality;

(v) If considered to have infringed the penal law, to have this decision and any measures imposed in consequence thereof reviewed by a higher competent, independent and impartial authority or judicial body according to law;

(vi) To have the free assistance of an interpreter if the child cannot understand or speak the language used;

(vii) To have his or her privacy fully respected at all stages of the proceedings.

3. States Parties shall seek to promote the establishment of laws, procedures, authorities and institutions specifically applicable to children alleged as, accused of, or recognized as having infringed the penal law, and, in particular:

(a) The establishment of a minimum age below which children shall be presumed not to have the capacity to infringe the penal law;

(b) Whenever appropriate and desirable, measures for dealing with such children without resorting to judicial proceedings, providing that human rights and legal safeguards are fully respected.

4. A variety of dispositions, such as care, guidance and supervision orders; counselling; probation; foster care; education and vocational training programmes and other alternatives to institutional care shall be available to ensure that children are dealt with in a manner appropriate to their well-being and proportionate both to their circumstances and the offence.

Article 41

Nothing in the present Convention shall affect any provisions which are more conducive to the realization of the rights of the child and which may be contained in:

(a) The law of a State Party; or

(b) International law in force for that State.

Part II

Article 42

States Parties undertake to make the principles and provisions of the Convention widely known, by appropriate and active means, to adults and children alike.

Article 43

1. For the purpose of examining the progress made by States Parties in achieving the realization of the obligations undertaken in the present Convention, there shall be established a Committee on the Rights of the Child, which shall carry out the functions hereinafter provided.

2. The Committee shall consist of ten experts of high moral standing and recognized competence in the field covered by this Convention. The members of the Committee shall be elected by States Parties from among their nationals and shall serve in their personal capacity, consideration being given to equitable geographical distribution, as well as to the principal legal systems.

3. The members of the Committee shall be elected by secret ballot from a list of persons nominated by States Parties. Each State Party may nominate one person from among its own nationals.

4. The initial election to the Committee shall be held no later than six months after the date of the entry into force of the present Convention and thereafter every second year. At least four months before the date of each election, the Secretary-General of the United Nations shall address a letter to States Parties inviting them to submit their nominations within two months. The Secretary-General shall subsequently prepare a list in alphabetical order of all persons thus nominated, indicating States Parties which have nominated them and shall submit it to the States Parties to the present Convention.

5. The elections shall be held at meetings of States Parties convened by the Secretary-General at United Nations Headquarters. At those meetings, for which two thirds of States Parties shall constitute a quorum, the persons elected to the Committee shall be those who obtain the largest number of votes and an absolute majority of the votes of the representatives of States Parties present and voting.

6. The members of the Committee shall be elected for a term of four years. They shall be eligible for re-election if renominated. The term of five of the members elected at the first election shall expire at the end of two years; immediately after the first election, the names of these five members shall be chosen by lot by the Chairman of the meeting.

7. If a member of the Committee dies or resigns or declares that for any other cause he or she can no longer perform the duties of the Committee, the State Party which nominated the member shall appoint another expert from among its nationals to serve for the remainder of the term, subject to the approval of the Committee.

8. The Committee shall establish its own rules of procedure.

9. The Committee shall elect its officers for a period of two years.

10. The meetings of the Committee shall normally be held at United Nations Headquarters or at any other convenient place as determined by the Committee. The Committee shall normally meet annually. The duration of the meetings of the Committee shall be determined and reviewed, if necessary, by a meeting of the States Parties to the present Convention, subject to the approval of the General Assembly.

11. The Secretary-General of the United Nations shall provide the necessary staff and facilities for the effective performance of the functions of the Committee under the present Convention.

12. With the approval of the General Assembly, the members of the Committee established under the present Convention shall receive emoluments from United Nations resources on such terms and conditions as the Assembly may decide.

Article 44

1. States Parties undertake to submit to the Committee, through the Secretary-General of the United Nations, reports on the measures they have adopted which give effect to the rights recognized herein and on the progress made on the enjoyment of those rights:

    (a) Within two years of the entry into force of the Convention for the State Party concerned;

    (b) Thereafter every five years.

2. Reports made under the present article shall indicate factors and difficulties, if any, affecting the degree of fulfilment of the obligations under the present Convention. Reports shall also contain sufficient information to provide the Committee with a comprehensive understanding of the implementation of the Convention in the country concerned.

3. A State Party which has submitted a comprehensive initial report to the Committee need not, in its subsequent reports submitted in accordance with paragraph 1 (b) of the present article, repeat basic information previously provided.

4. The Committee may request from States Parties further information relevant to the implementation of the Convention.

5. The Committee shall submit to the General Assembly, through the Economic and Social Council, every two years, reports on its activities.

6. States Parties shall make their reports widely available to the public in their own countries.

Article 45

In order to foster the effective implementation of the Convention and to encourage international co-operation in the field covered by the Convention:

    (a) The specialized agencies, the United Nations Chil-dren's Fund and other United Nations organs shall be entitled to be represented at the consideration of the implementation of such provisions of the present Convention as fall within the scope of their mandate. The Committee may invite the specialized agencies, the United Nations Children's Fund and other competent bodies as it may consider appropriate to provide expert advice on the implementation of the Convention in areas falling within the scope of their respective mandates. The Committee may invite the specialized agencies, the United Nations Children's Fund and other United Nations organs to submit reports on the implementation of the Convention in areas falling within the scope of their activities;

    (b) The Committee shall transmit, as it may consider appropriate, to the specialized agencies, the United Nations Children's Fund and other competent bodies, any reports from States Parties that contain a request, or indicate a need, for technical advice or assistance, along with the Committee's observations and suggestions, if any, on these requests or indications;

    (c) The Committee may recommend to the General Assembly to request the Secretary-General to undertake on its behalf studies on specific issues relating to the rights of the child;

    (d) The Committee may make suggestions and general recommendations based on information received pursuant to articles 44 and 45 of the present Convention. Such suggestions and general recommendations shall be transmitted to any State Party concerned and reported to the General Assembly, together with comments, if any, from States Parties.

PART III

Article 46

The present Convention shall be open for signature by all States.

Article 47

The present Convention is subject to ratification. Instruments of ratification shall be deposited with the Secretary-General of the United Nations.

Article 48

The present Convention shall remain open for accession by any State. The instruments of accession shall be deposited with the Secretary-General of the United Nations.

Article 49

1. The present Convention shall enter into force on the thirtieth day following the date of deposit with the Secretary-General of the United Nations of the twentieth instrument of ratification or accession.

2. For each State ratifying or acceding to the Convention after the deposit of the twentieth instrument of ratification or

accession, the Convention shall enter into force on the thirtieth day after the deposit by such State of its instrument of ratification or accession.

Article 50

1. Any State Party may propose an amendment and file it with the Secretary-General of the United Nations. The Secretary-General shall thereupon communicate the proposed amendment to States Parties, with a request that they indicate whether they favour a conference of States Parties for the purpose of considering and voting upon the proposals. In the event that, within four months from the date of such communication, at least one third of the States Parties favour such a conference, the Secretary-General shall convene the conference under the auspices of the United Nations. Any amendment adopted by a majority of States Parties present and voting at the conference shall be submitted to the General Assembly for approval.

2. An amendment adopted in accordance with paragraph 1 of the present article shall enter into force when it has been approved by the General Assembly of the United Nations and accepted by a two-thirds majority of States Parties.

3. When an amendment enters into force, it shall be binding on those States Parties which have accepted it, other States Parties still being bound by the provisions of the present Convention and any earlier amendments which they have accepted.

Article 51

1. The Secretary-General of the United Nations shall receive and circulate to all States the text of reservations made by States at the time of ratification or accession.

2. A reservation incompatible with the object and purpose of the present Convention shall not be permitted.

3. Reservations may be withdrawn at any time by notification to that effect addressed to the Secretary-General of the United Nations, who shall then inform all States. Such notification shall take effect on the date on which it is received by the Secretary-General.

Article 52

A State Party may denounce the present Convention by written notification to the Secretary-General of the United Nations. Denunciation becomes effective one year after the date of receipt of the notification by the Secretary-General.

Article 53

The Secretary-General of the United Nations is designated as the depositary of the present Convention.

Article 54

The original of the present Convention, of which the Arabic, Chinese, English, French, Russian and Spanish texts are equally authentic, shall be deposited with the Secretary-General of the United Nations.

In witness thereof the undersigned plenipotentiaries, being duly authorized thereto by their respective governments, have signed the present Convention.

Optional Protocol to the Convention on the Rights of the Child on the Sale of Children, Child Prostitution and Child Pornography

Entered into force, 18 January 2002.
The States Parties to the present Protocol,

Considering that, in order further to achieve the purposes of the Convention on the Rights of the Child and the implementation of its provisions, especially articles 1, 11, 21, 32, 33, 34, 35 and 36, it would be appropriate to extend the measures that States Parties should undertake in order to guarantee the protection of the child from the sale of children, child prostitution and child pornography,

Considering also that the Convention on the Rights of the Child recognizes the right of the child to be protected from economic exploitation and from performing any work that is likely to be hazardous or to interfere with the child's education, or to be harmful to the child's health or physical, mental, spiritual, moral or social development,

Gravely concerned at the significant and increasing international traffic in children for the purpose of the sale of children, child prostitution and child pornography,

Deeply concerned at the widespread and continuing practice of sex tourism, to which children are especially vulnerable, as it directly promotes the sale of children, child prostitution and child pornography,

Recognizing that a number of particularly vulnerable groups, including girl children, are at greater risk of sexual exploitation and that girl children are disproportionately represented among the sexually exploited,

Concerned about the growing availability of child pornography on the Internet and other evolving technologies, and recalling the International Conference on Combating Child Pornography on the Internet, held in Vienna in 1999, in particular its conclusion calling for the worldwide criminalization of the production, distribution, exportation, transmission, importation, intentional possession and advertising of child pornography, and stressing the importance of closer cooperation and partnership between Governments and the Internet industry,

Believing that the elimination of the sale of children, child prostitution and child pornography will be facilitated by adopting a holistic approach, addressing the contributing factors, including underdevelopment, poverty, economic disparities, inequitable socio-economic structure, dysfunctioning families, lack of education, urban-rural migration, gender discrimination, irresponsible adult sexual behaviour, harmful traditional practices, armed conflicts and trafficking in children,

Believing also that efforts to raise public awareness are needed to reduce consumer demand for the sale of children, child prostitution and child pornography, and believing further in the importance of strengthening global partnership among all actors and of improving law enforcement at the national level,

Noting the provisions of international legal instruments relevant to the protection of children, including the Hague Convention on Protection of Children and Cooperation in Respect of Intercountry Adoption, the Hague Convention on the Civil Aspects of International Child Abduction, the Hague Convention on Jurisdiction, Applicable Law, Recognition, Enforcement and Cooperation in Respect of Parental Responsibility and Measures for the Protection of Children, and International Labour Organization Convention No. 182 on the Prohibition and Immediate Action for the Elimination of the Worst Forms of Child Labour,

Encouraged by the overwhelming support for the Convention on the Rights of the Child, demonstrating the widespread commitment that exists for the promotion and protection of the rights of the child,

Recognizing the importance of the implementation of the provisions of the Programme of Action for the Prevention of the Sale of Children, Child Prostitution and Child Pornography and the Declaration and Agenda for Action adopted at the World Congress against Commercial Sexual Exploitation of Children, held in Stockholm from 27 to 31 August 1996, and the other relevant decisions and recommendations of pertinent international bodies,

Taking due account of the importance of the traditions and cultural values of each people for the protection and harmonious development of the child,

Have agreed as follows:

Article 1

States Parties shall prohibit the sale of children, child prostitution and child pornography as provided for by the present Protocol.

Article 2

For the purposes of the present Protocol:
- (a) Sale of children means any act or transaction whereby a child is transferred by any person or group of persons to another for remuneration or any other consideration;
- (b) Child prostitution means the use of a child in sexual activities for remuneration or any other form of consideration;
- (c) Child pornography means any representation, by whatever means, of a child engaged in real or simulated explicit sexual activities or any representation of the sexual parts of a child for primarily sexual purposes.

Article 3

1. Each State Party shall ensure that, as a minimum, the following acts and activities are fully covered under its criminal or penal law, whether such offences are committed domestically or transnationally or on an individual or organized basis:
   - (a) In the context of sale of children as defined in article 2:
     - (i) Offering, delivering or accepting, by whatever means, a child for the purpose of:
       - a. Sexual exploitation of the child;
       - b. Transfer of organs of the child for profit;
       - c. Engagement of the child in forced labour;
     - (ii) Improperly inducing consent, as an intermediary, for the adoption of a child in violation of applicable international legal instruments on adoption;
   - (b) Offering, obtaining, procuring or providing a child for child prostitution, as defined in article 2;
   - (c) Producing, distributing, disseminating, importing, exporting, offering, selling or possessing for the above purposes child pornography as defined in article 2.
2. Subject to the provisions of the national law of a State Party, the same shall apply to an attempt to commit any of the said acts and to complicity or participation in any of the said acts.
3. Each State Party shall make such offences punishable by appropriate penalties that take into account their grave nature.
4. Subject to the provisions of its national law, each State Party shall take measures, where appropriate, to establish the liability of legal persons for offences established in paragraph 1 of the present article. Subject to the legal principles of the State Party, such liability of legal persons may be criminal, civil or administrative.
5. States Parties shall take all appropriate legal and administrative measures to ensure that all persons involved in the adoption of a child act in conformity with applicable international legal instruments.

Article 4

1. Each State Party shall take such measures as may be necessary to establish its jurisdiction over the offences referred to in article 3, paragraph 1, when the offences are commited in its territory or on board a ship or aircraft registered in that State.
2. Each State Party may take such measures as may be necessary to establish its jurisdiction over the offences referred to in article 3, paragraph 1, in the following cases:

(a) When the alleged offender is a national of that State or a person who has his habitual residence in its territory;

(b) When the victim is a national of that State.

3. Each State Party shall also take such measures as may be necessary to establish its jurisdiction over the aforementioned offences when the alleged offender is present in its territory and it does not extradite him or her to another State Party on the ground that the offence has been committed by one of its nationals.

4. The present Protocol does not exclude any criminal jurisdiction exercised in accordance with internal law.

Article 5

1. The offences referred to in article 3, paragraph 1, shall be deemed to be included as extraditable offences in any extradition treaty existing between States Parties and shall be included as extraditable offences in every extradition treaty subsequently concluded between them, in accordance with the conditions set forth in such treaties.

2. If a State Party that makes extradition conditional on the existence of a treaty receives a request for extradition from another State Party with which it has no extradition treaty, it may consider the present Protocol to be a legal basis for extradition in respect of such offences. Extradition shall be subject to the conditions provided by the law of the requested State.

3. States Parties that do not make extradition conditional on the existence of a treaty shall recognize such offences as extraditable offences between themselves subject to the conditions provided by the law of the requested State.

4. Such offences shall be treated, for the purpose of extradition between States Parties, as if they had been committed not only in the place in which they occurred but also in the territories of the States required to establish their jurisdiction in accordance with article 4.

5. If an extradition request is made with respect to an offence described in article 3, paragraph 1, and the requested State Party does not or will not extradite on the basis of the nationality of the offender, that State shall take suitable measures to submit the case to its competent authorities for the purpose of prosecution.

Article 6

1. States Parties shall afford one another the greatest measure of assistance in connection with investigations or criminal or extradition proceedings brought in respect of the offences set forth in article 3, paragraph 1, including assistance in obtaining evidence at their disposal necessary for the proceedings.

2. States Parties shall carry out their obligations under paragraph 1 of the present article in conformity with any treaties or other arrangements on mutual legal assistance that may exist between them. In the absence of such treaties or arrangements, States Parties shall afford one another assistance in accordance with their domestic law.

Article 7

States Parties shall, subject to the provisions of their national law:

(a) Take measures to provide for the seizure and confiscation, as appropriate, of:

(i) Goods, such as materials, assets and other instrumentalities used to commit or facilitate offences under the present protocol;

(ii) Proceeds derived from such offences;

(b) Execute requests from another State Party for seizure or confiscation of goods or proceeds referred to in subparagraph (a);

(c) Take measures aimed at closing, on a temporary or definitive basis, premises used to commit such offences.

Article 8

1. States Parties shall adopt appropriate measures to protect the rights and interests of child victims of the practices prohibited under the present Protocol at all stages of the criminal justice process, in particular by:

(a) Recognizing the vulnerability of child victims and adapting procedures to recognize their special needs, including their special needs as witnesses;

(b) Informing child victims of their rights, their role and the scope, timing and progress of the proceedings and of the disposition of their cases;

(c) Allowing the views, needs and concerns of child victims to be presented and considered in proceedings where their personal interests are affected, in a manner consistent with the procedural rules of national law;

(d) Providing appropriate support services to child victims throughout the legal process;

(e) Protecting, as appropriate, the privacy and identity of child victims and taking measures in accordance with national law to avoid the inappropriate dissemination of information that could lead to the identification of child victims;

(f) Providing, in appropriate cases, for the safety of child victims, as well as that of their families and witnesses on their behalf, from intimidation and retaliation;

(g) Avoiding unnecessary delay in the disposition of cases and the execution of orders or decrees granting compensation to child victims.

2. States Parties shall ensure that uncertainty as to the actual age of the victim shall not prevent the initiation of criminal investigations, including investigations aimed at establishing the age of the victim.

3. States Parties shall ensure that, in the treatment by the criminal justice system of children who are victims of the offences described in the present Protocol, the best interest of the child shall be a primary consideration.

4. States Parties shall take measures to ensure appropriate training, in particular legal and psychological training, for the persons who work with victims of the offences prohibited under the present Protocol.

5. States Parties shall, in appropriate cases, adopt measures in order to protect the safety and integrity of those persons and/or organizations involved in the prevention and/or protection and rehabilitation of victims of such offences.

6. Nothing in the present article shall be construed to be prejudicial to or inconsistent with the rights of the accused to a fair and impartial trial.

Article 9

1. States Parties shall adopt or strengthen, implement and disseminate laws, administrative measures, social policies and programmes to prevent the offences referred to in the present Protocol. Particular attention shall be given to protect children who are especially vulnerable to such practices.

2. States Parties shall promote awareness in the public at large, including children, through information by all appropriate means, education and training, about the preventive measures and harmful effects of the offences referred to in the present Protocol. In fulfilling their obligations under this article, States Parties shall encourage the participation of the community and, in particular, children and child victims, in such information and education and training programmes, including at the international level.

3. States Parties shall take all feasible measures with the aim of ensuring all appropriate assistance to victims of such offences, including their full social reintegration and their full physical and psychological recovery.

4. States Parties shall ensure that all child victims of the offences described in the present Protocol have access to adequate procedures to seek, without discrimination, compensation for damages from those legally responsible.

5. States Parties shall take appropriate measures aimed at effectively prohibiting the production and dissemination of material advertising the offences described in the present Protocol.

Article 10

1. States Parties shall take all necessary steps to strengthen international cooperation by multilateral, regional and bilateral arrangements for the prevention, detection, investigation, prosecution and punishment of those responsible for acts involving the sale of children, child prostitution, child pornography and child sex tourism. States Parties shall also promote international cooperation and coordination between their authorities, national and international non-governmental organizations and international organizations.

2. States Parties shall promote international cooperation to assist child victims in their physical and psychological recovery, social reintegration and repatriation.

3. States Parties shall promote the strengthening of international cooperation in order to address the root causes, such as poverty and underdevelopment, contributing to the vulnerability of children to the sale of children, child prostitution, child pornography and child sex tourism.

4. States Parties in a position to do so shall provide financial, technical or other assistance through existing multilateral, regional, bilateral or other programmes.

Article 11

Nothing in the present Protocol shall affect any provisions that are more conducive to the realization of the rights of the child and that may be contained in:

(a) The law of a State Party;

(b) International law in force for that State.

Article 12

1. Each State Party shall, within two years following the entry into force of the present Protocol for that State Party, submit a report to the Committee on the Rights of the Child providing comprehensive information on the measures it has taken to implement the provisions of the Protocol.

2. Following the submission of the comprehensive report, each State Party shall include in the reports they submit to the Committee on the Rights of the Child, in accordance with article 44 of the Convention, any further information with respect to the implementation of the present Protocol. Other States Parties to the Protocol shall submit a report every five years.

3. The Committee on the Rights of the Child may request from States Parties further information relevant to the implementation of the present Protocol.

Article 13

1. The present Protocol is open for signature by any State that is a party to the Convention or has signed it.

2. The present Protocol is subject to ratification and is open to accession by any State that is a party to the Convention or has signed it. Instruments of ratification or accession shall be deposited with the Secretary-General of the United Nations.

Article 14

1. The present Protocol shall enter into force three months after the deposit of the tenth instrument of ratification or accession.

2. For each State ratifying the present Protocol or acceding to it after its entry into force, the Protocol shall enter into force one month after the date of the deposit of its own instrument of ratification or accession.

Article 15

1. Any State Party may denounce the present Protocol at any time by written notification to the Secretary-General of the United Nations, who shall thereafter inform the other States Parties to the Convention and all States that have signed the Convention. The denunciation shall take effect one year after the date of receipt of the notification by the Secretary-General.

2. Such a denunciation shall not have the effect of releasing the State Party from its obligations under the present Protocol in regard to any offence that occurs prior to the date on which the

denunciation becomes effective. Nor shall such a denunciation prejudice in any way the continued consideration of any matter that is already under consideration by the Committee on the Rights of the Child prior to the date on which the denunciation becomes effective.

Article 16

1. Any State Party may propose an amendment and file it with the Secretary-General of the United Nations. The Secretary-General shall thereupon communicate the proposed amendment to States Parties with a request that they indicate whether they favour a conference of States Parties for the purpose of considering and voting upon the proposals. In the event that, within four months from the date of such communication, at least one third of the States Parties favour such a conference, the Secretary-General shall convene the conference under the auspices of the United Nations. Any amendment adopted by a majority of States Parties present and voting at the conference shall be submitted to the General Assembly of the United Nations for approval.
2. An amendment adopted in accordance with paragraph 1 of the present article shall enter into force when it has been approved by the General Assembly and accepted by a two-thirds majority of States Parties.
3. When an amendment enters into force, it shall be binding on those States Parties that have accepted it, other States Parties still being bound by the provisions of the present Protocol and any earlier amendments they have accepted.

Article 17

1. The present Protocol, of which the Arabic, Chinese, English, French, Russian and Spanish texts are equally authentic, shall be deposited in the archives of the United Nations.
2. The Secretary-General of the United Nations shall transmit certified copies of the present Protocol to all States Parties to the Convention and all States that have signed the Convention.

Optional Protocol to the Convention on the Rights of the Child on the Involvement of Children in Armed Conflict

Entered into force, 12 February 2002.
The States Parties to the present Protocol,

Encouraged by the overwhelming support for the Convention on the Rights of the Child, demonstrating the widespread commitment that exists to strive for the promotion and protection of the rights of the child,

Reaffirming that the rights of children require special protection, and calling for continuous improvement of the situation of children without distinction, as well as for their development and education in conditions of peace and security,

Disturbed by the harmful and widespread impact of armed conflict on children and the long-term consequences it has for durable peace, security and development,

Condemning the targeting of children in situations of armed conflict and direct attacks on objects protected under international law, including places that generally have a significant presence of children, such as schools and hospitals,

Noting the adoption of the Rome Statute of the International Criminal Court, in particular, the inclusion therein as a war crime, of conscripting or enlisting children under the age of 15 years or using them to participate actively in hostilities in both international and non-international armed conflicts,

Considering therefore that to strengthen further the implementation of rights recognized in the Convention on the Rights of the Child there is a need to increase the protection of children from involvement in armed conflict,

Noting that article 1 of the Convention on the Rights of the Child specifies that, for the purposes of that Convention, a child means every human being below the age of 18 years unless, under the law applicable to the child, majority is attained earlier,

Convinced that an optional protocol to the Convention that raises the age of possible recruitment of persons into armed forces and their participation in hostilities will contribute effectively to the implementation of the principle that the best interests of the child are to be a primary consideration in all actions concerning children,

Noting that the twenty-sixth International Conference of the Red Cross and Red Crescent in December 1995 recommended, *inter alia*, that parties to conflict take every feasible step to ensure that children below the age of 18 years do not take part in hostilities,

Welcoming the unanimous adoption, in June 1999, of International Labour Organization Convention No. 182 on the Prohibition and Immediate Action for the Elimination of the Worst Forms of Child Labour, which prohibits, *inter alia*, forced or compulsory recruitment of children for use in armed conflict,

Condemning with the gravest concern the recruitment, training and use within and across national borders of children in hostilities by armed groups distinct from the armed forces of a State, and recognizing the responsibility of those who recruit, train and use children in this regard,

Recalling the obligation of each party to an armed conflict to abide by the provisions of international humanitarian law,

Stressing that the present Protocol is without prejudice to the purposes and principles contained in the Charter of the United Nations, including Article 51, and relevant norms of humanitarian law,

Bearing in mind that conditions of peace and security based on full respect of the purposes and principles contained in the Charter and observance of applicable human rights instruments are indispensable for the full protection of children, in particular during armed conflicts and foreign occupation,

Recognizing the special needs of those children who are particularly vulnerable to recruitment or use in hostilities contrary to the present Protocol owing to their economic or social status or gender,

Mindful of the necessity of taking into consideration the economic, social and political root causes of the involvement of children in armed conflicts,

Convinced of the need to strengthen international cooperation in the implementation of the present Protocol, as well as the physical and psychosocial rehabilitation and social reintegration of children who are victims of armed conflict,

Encouraging the participation of the community and, in particular, children and child victims in the dissemination of informational and educational programmes concerning the implementation of the Protocol,

Have agreed as follows:

Article 1

States Parties shall take all feasible measures to ensure that members of their armed forces who have not attained the age of 18 years do not take a direct part in hostilities.

Article 2

States Parties shall ensure that persons who have not attained the age of 18 years are not compulsorily recruited into their armed forces.

Article 3

1. States Parties shall raise in years the minimum age for the voluntary recruitment of persons into their national armed forces from that set out in article 38, paragraph 3, of the Convention on the Rights of the Child, taking account of the principles contained in that article and recognizing that under the Convention persons under the age of 18 years are entitled to special protection.

2. Each State Party shall deposit a binding declaration upon ratification of or accession to the present Protocol that sets forth the minimum age at which it will permit voluntary recruitment into its national armed forces and a description of the safeguards it has adopted to ensure that such recruitment is not forced or coerced.

3. States Parties that permit voluntary recruitment into their national armed forces under the age of 18 years shall maintain safeguards to ensure, as a minimum, that:
   (a) Such recruitment is genuinely voluntary;
   (b) Such recruitment is carried out with the informed consent of the person's parents or legal guardians;
   (c) Such persons are fully informed of the duties involved in such military service;
   (d) Such persons provide reliable proof of age prior to acceptance into national military service.

4. Each State Party may strengthen its declaration at any time by notification to that effect addressed to the Secretary-General of the United Nations, who shall inform all States Parties. Such notification shall take effect on the date on which it is received by the Secretary-General.

5. The requirement to raise the age in paragraph 1 of the present article does not apply to schools operated by or under the control of the armed forces of the States Parties, in keeping with articles 28 and 29 of the Convention on the Rights of the Child.

Article 4

1. Armed groups that are distinct from the armed forces of a State should not, under any circumstances, recruit or use in hostilities persons under the age of 18 years.

2. States Parties shall take all feasible measures to prevent such recruitment and use, including the adoption of legal measures necessary to prohibit and criminalize such practices.

3. The application of the present article shall not affect the legal status of any party to an armed conflict.

Article 5

Nothing in the present Protocol shall be construed as precluding provisions in the law of a State Party or in international instruments and international humanitarian law that are more conducive to the realization of the rights of the child.

Article 6

1. Each State Party shall take all necessary legal, administrative and other measures to ensure the effective implementation and enforcement of the provisions of the present Protocol within its jurisdiction.

2. States Parties undertake to make the principles and provisions of the present Protocol widely known and promoted by appropriate means, to adults and children alike.

3. States Parties shall take all feasible measures to ensure that persons within their jurisdiction recruited or used in hostilities con-

trary to the present Protocol are demobilized or otherwise released from service. States Parties shall, when necessary, accord to such persons all appropriate assistance for their physical and psychological recovery and their social reintegration.

Article 7

1. States Parties shall cooperate in the implementation of the present Protocol, including in the prevention of any activity contrary thereto and in the rehabilitation and social reintegration of persons who are victims of acts contrary thereto, including through technical cooperation and financial assistance. Such assistance and cooperation will be undertaken in consultation with the States Parties concerned and the relevant international organizations.
2. States Parties in a position to do so shall provide such assistance through existing multilateral, bilateral or other programmes or, *inter alia*, through a voluntary fund established in accordance with the rules of the General Assembly.

Article 8

1. Each State Party shall, within two years following the entry into force of the present Protocol for that State Party, submit a report to the Committee on the Rights of the Child providing comprehensive information on the measures it has taken to implement the provisions of the Protocol, including the measures taken to implement the provisions on participation and recruitment.
2. Following the submission of the comprehensive report, each State Party shall include in the reports it submits to the Committee on the Rights of the Child, in accordance with article 44 of the Convention, any further information with respect to the implementation of the Protocol. Other States Parties to the Protocol shall submit a report every five years.
3. The Committee on the Rights of the Child may request from States Parties further information relevant to the implementation of the present Protocol.

Article 9

1. The present Protocol is open for signature by any State that is a party to the Convention or has signed it.
2. The present Protocol is subject to ratification and is open to accession by any State. Instruments of ratification or accession shall be deposited with the Secretary-General of the United Nations.
3. The Secretary-General, in his capacity as depositary of the Convention and the Protocol, shall inform all States Parties to the Convention and all States that have signed the Convention of each instrument of declaration pursuant to article 3.

Article 10

1. The present Protocol shall enter into force three months after the deposit of the tenth instrument of ratification or accession.
2. For each State ratifying the present Protocol or acceding to it after its entry into force, the Protocol shall enter into force one month after the date of the deposit of its own instrument of ratification or accession.

Article 11

1. Any State Party may denounce the present Protocol at any time by written notification to the Secretary-General of the United Nations, who shall thereafter inform the other States Parties to the Convention and all States that have signed the Convention. The denunciation shall take effect one year after the date of receipt of the notification by the Secretary-General. If, however, on the expiry of that year the denouncing State Party is engaged in armed conflict, the denunciation shall not take effect before the end of the armed conflict.
2. Such a denunciation shall not have the effect of releasing the State Party from its obligations under the present Protocol in regard to any act that occurs prior to the date on which the denunciation becomes effective. Nor shall such a denunciation prejudice in any way the continued consideration of any matter that is already under consideration by the Committee on the Rights of the Child prior to the date on which the denunciation becomes effective.

Article 12

1. Any State Party may propose an amendment and file it with the Secretary-General of the United Nations. The Secretary-General shall thereupon communicate the proposed amendment to States Parties with a request that they indicate whether they favour a conference of States Parties for the purpose of considering and voting upon the proposals. In the event that, within four months from the date of such communication, at least one third of the States Parties favour such a conference, the Secretary-General shall convene the conference under the auspices of the United Nations. Any amendment adopted by a majority of States Parties present and voting at the conference shall be submitted to the General Assembly of the United Nations for approval.
2. An amendment adopted in accordance with paragraph 1 of the present article shall enter into force when it has been approved by the General Assembly and accepted by a two-thirds majority of States Parties.
3. When an amendment enters into force, it shall be binding on those States Parties that have accepted it, other States Parties still being bound by the provisions of the present Protocol and any earlier amendments they have accepted.

Article 13

1. The present Protocol, of which the Arabic, Chinese, English, French, Russian and Spanish texts are equally authentic, shall be deposited in the archives of the United Nations.
2. The Secretary-General of the United Nations shall transmit certified copies of the present Protocol to all States Parties to the Convention and all States that have signed the Conventions.

References

CHAPTER 1

[1] International Labour Organization, 'Origins and History', <www.ilo.org/global/About_the_ILO/Origins_and_history/lang-en/index.htm>, Night Work of Young Persons (Industry) Convention , 1919, <www.ilo.org/ilolex/cgi-lex/convde.pl?C006>, Minimum Age (Agriculture) Convention, 1921, <www.ilo.org/ilolex/cgilex/convde.pl?C010>, ILO, Geneva, accessed 16 July 2009.

[2] International Committee of the Red Cross, 'International Review of the Red Cross', May 1963, no. 26, pp. 227–228, <www.loc.gov/rr/frd/Military_Law/pdf/RC_May-1963.pdf>, accessed 16 July 2009.

[3] Save the Children Fund archive reference SC/SF/17, cited in United Nations Children's Fund, *The State of the World's Children 2000: A vision for the 21st century*, UNICEF, New York, 1999, p. 14.

[4] League of Nations, Geneva Declaration of the Rights of the Child, 26 September 1924, <www.un-documents.net/gdrc1924.htm>, accessed 16 July 2009.

[5] United Nations, Declaration of the Rights of the Child, 20 November 1959, <www.unhchr.ch/html/menu3/b/25.htm>, accessed 16 July 2009.

[5] United Nations Children's Fund, *Progress for Children: A report card on child protection*, Number 8, UNICEF, New York (forthcoming September 2009).

[7] United Nations Children's Fund, *The State of the World's Children 2009: Maternal and newborn health*, UNICEF, New York, December 2008, p. 23.

[8] United Nations Children's Fund, *Children and AIDS: Third stocktaking report*, UNICEF, New York, 2008, p. 16.

[9] United Nations Children's Fund, *Progress for Children: A report card on child protection*, Number 8, UNICEF, New York (forthcoming September 2009).

[10] Filmer, Deon, 'Disability, Poverty and Schooling in Developing Countries: Results from 11 household surveys', *World Bank Policy Research Paper 3794*, Washington, D.C., December 2005, p. 15; Sobsey, Dick, 'Exceptionality, Education, and Maltreatment', *Exceptionality*, vol. 10, no. 1, 2002, pp. 29–46.

[11] United Nations Children's Fund, *Progress for Children: A report card on child protection*, Number 8, UNICEF, New York (forthcoming September 2009).

[12] Gillespie, Stuart, 'Food Prices and the AIDS Response: How they are linked, and what can be done', HIV, Livelihoods, Food and Nutrition Security: Findings from RENE WAL Research (2007–2008), Brief 1, International Food Policy Research Institute, 2008.

[13] Lansdown, Gerison, *The Evolving Capacities of the Child*, *Innocenti Insight*, UNICEF Innocenti Research Centre, Florence, 2005, pp. ix, 3–7.

[14] United Nations Children's Fund, *The State of the World's Children 2006: Excluded and invisible*, UNICEF, New York, December 2005, p. 67.

[15] Lerner, Josh, and Estair Van Wagner, 'Participatory Budgeting in Canada: Democratic innovations in strategic spaces', Transnational Institute, Amsterdam, February 2006, <www.tni.org/detail_page.phtml?page=newpol-docs_pbcanada>, accessed 30 June 2009.

[16] www.participatorybudgeting.org.uk/case-studies/the-childrens-fund-newcastle; National Youth Agency, *Young People's Involvement in Participatory Budgeting*, www.nya.org.uk/shared_asp_files/GFSR.asp?NodeID=113044.

[17] ECPAT International, 'Ensuring Meaningful Child and Youth Participation in the Fight against Commercial Sexual Exploitation of Children: The ECPAT experience', ECPAT International, Bangkok, October 2007; Feinstein, Clare, Ravi Karkara and Theodore Talbot, 'Act Now! Some highlights from children's participation in the regional consultations for the UN Study on Violence against Children', Save the Children, London, 2005, p. 9); Committee on the Rights of the Child, 'Day of General Discussion on the Right to Be Heard', 2006, cited in Feinstein, Clare, and Claire O'Kane, 'Children and Adolescents' Participation and Protection from Sexual Abuse and Exploitation', *UNICEF Innocenti Working Paper, IWP 2009-09*, United Nations Children's Fund, Florence, February 2009, p. 1.

[18] Feinstein, Clare, and Claire O'Kane, 'Children and Adolescents' Participation and Protection from Sexual Abuse and Exploitation', *UNICEF Innocenti Working Paper, IWP 2009-09*, United Nations Children's Fund, Florence, February 2009, p. 1.

CHAPTER 1 PANELS

The evolution of international standards on child rights

United Nations Children's Fund, *The State of the World's Children 2005: Childhood under threat*, UNICEF, New York, December 2004, p. 2.

Optional Protocols to the Convention

Office of the United Nations High Commissioner for Human Rights, <www2.ohchr.org/english/law/crc-sale.htm>, accessed 30 June 2009; Stohl, Rachel, 'Children in conflict: Assessing the Optional Protocol', *Journal of Conflict, Security and Development*, vol. 2, no. 2, 2002, p. 138.

The Committee on the Rights of the Child

Office of the United Nations High Commissioner for Human Rights, <www2.ohchr.org/english/bodies/treaty/>, accessed 30 June 2009.

General Comments of the Committee on the Rights of the Child and general measures of implementation of the Convention

Office of the United Nations High Commissioner for Human Rights, <www2.ohchr.org/english/bodies/CRC>, accessed 30 June 2009; General Comment No. 5: General Measures of Implementation (articles. 4, 42, 44, para. 6), October 2003; Newell, Peter, 'Legal Frameworks for Combating Sexual Exploitation of Children', UNICEF Innocenti Research Centre Working Paper, p. 5, <www.unicef-irc.org/knowledge_pages/resource_pages/worldcongress3/bern_consultation/newell.pdf>, accessed 30 June 2009.

The human rights-based approach to programming for women and children

United Nations, 'The Human Rights Based Approach to Development Cooperation: Towards a common understanding among UN agencies'; United Nations Children's Fund, 'A Human Rights Approach to UNICEF Programming for Children and Women: What it is, and some changes it will bring', Guidelines for human rights-based programming approach, CF/EXD/1998-04 of 21 April 1998, pp. 8, 16; Goonesekere, Savitri, and Rangita de Silva-De Alwis, 'Women's and Children's Rights in a Human Rights Based Approach to Development', *UNICEF Working Paper*, Division of Policy and Planning, New York, September 2005, pp. 1–2, 17, 41, 43; Rozga, Dorothy, 'Applying a Human Rights Based Approach to Programming: Experiences of UNICEF', United Nations Children's Fund, Presentation paper prepared for the Workshop on Human Rights, Assets and Livelihood Security, and Sustainable Development, June 2001, pp. 2, 5-8. Lechtig, Aarón et al., 'Decreasing stunting, anemia, and vitamin A deficiency in Peru: Results of The Good Start in Life Programme', *Food and Nutrition Bulletin,* vol. 20, no. 1, United Nations University, pp. 37-45.

Child rights in South Africa

Government of the Republic of South Africa, 'Constitution of the Republic of South Africa', Chapter 2, Johannesburg, 1996, <www.info.gov.za/documents/constitution/1996/96cons2.htm#28>, accessed 20 April 2009; Government of the Republic of South Africa, 'Children's Act (No. 38 of 2005)', *Government Gazette*, vol. 492, no. 28944, 19 June 2006, and 'Children's Amendment Act (No. 41 of 2007)', *Government Gazette*, vol. 513, no. 30884, 18 March 2008; Economist Intelligence Unit, South Africa Country Profile, EIU, London, 2008, p. 17; United Nations Children's Fund, *The State of the World's Children 2009: Maternal and newborn health*, UNICEF, New York, December 2008, p. 132; Geffen, Nathan, 'What Do South Africa's AIDS Statistics Mean? A TAC briefing paper', Treatment Action Campaign, Cape Town, 7 August 2006, <www.tac.org.za/community/aidsstats>, accessed 20 April 2009; 'Children's Charter of South Africa', African National Congress, Johannesburg, 1 June 1992, <www.anc.org.za/misc/childcht.html>, accessed 21 April 2009.

Progress on survival and development rights/Challenges of survival and development/Challenges of disparities/Challenges of protection

Figures derived from UNICEF global database, 2009, and Child Info, <www.childinfo.org>, accessed 30 June 2009.

Child rights in China

World Bank, *From Poor Areas to Poor People: China's evolving poverty reduction agenda – An assessment of poverty and inequality in China*, The World Bank Office, Beijing, March 2009, p. iii; Tang, Shenglan, et al., 'Tackling the Challenges to Health Equity in China', *The Lancet*, vol. 372, no. 9648, 25 October 2008, p. 1494; National Bureau of Statistics of China, '1% National Population Sample Survey of 2005', NBS, Beijing, 22 March 2006; National Working Committee on Children and Women under the State Council, 'Presentation to the 2008 UNICEF Mid-Term Review' (figure derived from '1% National Population Sample Survey of 2005'), NWCCW, Beijing, 2008; Population Research Centre of Renmin University of China, 'Population Research No. 3' (figure derived from '1% National Population Sample Survey of 2005'), Renmin University, Beijing, 2008; National Bureau of Statistics of China, Figures derived from '1% National Population Sample Survey of 2005'), Beijing, 2007; United Nations Children's Fund, *UNICEF China Annual Report 2008*, UNICEF China, Beijing, 2009, p. 7.

Child rights in Egypt

Economist Intelligence Unit, Egypt Country Profile, EIU, London, 2008, pp. 3, 14; Save the Children, *State of the World's Mothers 2007: Saving the lives of children under 5*, Save the Children, Westport, CT, May 2007, p. 22; United Nations Children's Fund, 'The Situation of Children and Women in Egypt', UNICEF Egypt, Cairo, <www.unicef.org/egypt/overview.html>, accessed 26 May 2009; United Nations Development Programme and Institute of National Planning, *Egypt Human*

Development Report 2008: Egypt's social contract – The role of civil society, UNDP and Institute of National Planning, New York and Cairo, 2008, pp. 39–43, 50; United Nations Children's Fund, Yamamah, Gamel Abdel Nasser, et al., 'Health Profile of Bedouin Children Living at South Sinai', *Journal of Medical Science*, vol. 7, no. 6 , 15 August 2007, p. 1013; Tag-Eldin, Mohammed A., et al., 'Prevalence of Female Genital Cutting among Egyptian Girls', *Bulletin of the World Health Organization*, vol. 86, no. 4, April 2008, p. 271; Hassanin, Ibrahim M. A., 'Prevalence of Female Genital Cutting in Upper Egypt: 6 years after enforcement of prohibition law', *Ethics, Bioscience and Life*, vol. 16 (supplement 1), March 2008, p. 30; Stack, Liam, 'United Nations Development Programme and Institute of National Planning, *Egypt Human Development Report 2008: Egypt's social contract – The role of civil society*, UNDP and Institute of National Planning, New York and Cairo, 2008, p. 210; Nile Basin Initiative website, <www.nilebasin.org>, accessed 27 March 2009.

The Convention's impact on public and private institutions

United Nations Children's Fund, 'Global Perspectives on Consolidated Children's Rights Statutes', *Legislative Reform Initiative Paper Series*, UNICEF, Division of Policy and Practice, September 2008, pp. ii–iii, 13, 20, 36; United Nations Children's Fund, *The State of the World's Children 2006: Excluded and invisible*, UNICEF, New York, December 2005, pp. 66–81; Gore, Radhika, and Alberto Minujin, Background Note: Budget initiatives for children, Global Policy Section, Division of Policy and Planning, UNICEF, New York, 2003; Jonsson, Urban, 'Human Rights Approach to Development Programming', Eastern and Southern Africa Regional Office UNICEF, 2003; African Charter on the Rights and Welfare of the Child, OAU Doc. CAB/LEG/24.9/49 (1990); UN Committee on the Rights of the Child, 'The Private Sector As Service Provider and Its Role in Implementing Children's Rights', Office of the High Commissioner for Human Rights, Geneva, 2002; United Nations Children's Fund, 'Principles and Guidelines for Ethical Reporting: Children and young people under 18 years old', New York; United Nations Children's Fund, *What Religious Leaders Can Do About HIV/AIDS: Actions for Children and Young People*, UNICEF, New York, 2003; United Nations Children's Fund, *Building Trust in Immunization: Partnering with religious leaders and groups*, UNICEF, New York, May 2004.

Child rights in Sierra Leone

Government of Sierra Leone, 'The Child Rights Act, 2007', *Sierra Leone Gazette Extraordinary*, vol. CXXXVIII (supplement), no. 43, 3 September 2007, <www.sierra-leone.org/Laws/2007-7p.pdf>, accessed 28 May 2009; United Nations Development Programme, *Human Development Report 2007/2008: Fighting climate change – Human solidarity in a divided world*, UNDP, New York, 2007, p. 232; United Nations Children's Fund, *The State of the World's Children 2009: Maternal and newborn health*, UNICEF, New York, 2008, pp. 120, 128.

Child Friendly Cities: An international initiative promoting child participation in local government

UNICEF Innocenti Research Centre, *Building Child Friendly Cities: A framework for action*, UNICEF IRC, Florence, 2004, pp. 1, 4; Riggio, Eliana, 'Child Friendly Cities: Good governance in the best interest of the child', *Environment and Urbanization*, vol. 14, no. 2, October 2002, p. 54; UNICEF Innocenti Research Centre, Child Friendly Cities Database, <www.childfriendlycities.org/networking/index_examples.html>, accessed 30 June 2009; Corsi, Marco, 'The Child Friendly Cities Initiatives in Italy', *Journal of Environment and Urbanization*, Vol.14, No. 2,October 2002.

Child rights in India

Asian Centre for Human Rights, 'South Asia Human Rights Index 2008', New Delhi, pp. 7, 16; United Nations Children's Fund, *The State of the World's*

Children 2009: Maternal and newborn health, UNICEF, New York, December 2008, p. 85; Indian Medical Association Newsletter, December 2007–January 2008, pp.16–17; Economist Intelligence Unit, India Country Forecast, April 2009, EIU, London, 2009, p. 9; Durand, Tina M., and M. Brinton Lykes, 'Think Globally, Act Locally: A global perspective on mobilizing adults for positive youth development', Chapter 13, *Mobilizing Adults for Positive Youth Development: Strategies for closing the gaps between beliefs and behaviors*, edited by E. Gil and Jean E. Rhodes, Springer, 2006, pp. 242–243.

CHAPTER 2

The essays on the Convention presented in this chapter represent the personal perspectives, findings, interpretations and conclusions of the authors and do not necessarily reflect the positions of the United Nations Children's Fund.

CHAPTER 3

[1] Derived from United Nations Population Division, 'World Population Prospects: The 2008 Revision – Population Database', <http://esa.un.org/unpp/>, accessed 16 June 2009.

[2] Dobie, Philip, et al., 'How Do Poor People Adapt to Weather Variability and Natural Disasters Today?', *Human Development Report Office Occasional Paper, 2007/24*, United Nations Development Programme, New York, 2008, pp. 12–22

[3] United Nations Children's Fund, *The State of the World's Children 2008: Child survival*, UNICEF, New York, December 2007, pp. 29–30.

[4] United Nations Children's Fund, *The State of the World's Children 1996*, UNICEF, New York, December 1995, pp. 59–60.

[5] Belli, Paolo C., Flavia Bustreo and Alexander Preker, 'Investing in Children's Health: What are the economic benefits?', *Bulletin of the World Health Organization*, vol. 83, no. 10, October 2005, pp. 777–784; Grantham-McGregor, Sally, et al., 'Developmental Potential in the First 5 Years for Children in Developing Countries', *The Lancet*, vol. 369, no. 9555, January 2007, pp. 60–70.

CHAPTER 3 PANELS

The global economic crisis: Implications for child rights

Alderman, Harold, John Hoddinott and Bill Kinsey, 'Long Term Consequences of Early Childhood Malnutrition', *Oxford Economic Papers*, Oxford University Press, vol. 58, no. 3, 2006, pp. 450–474; Baird, Sarah, Jed Friedman and Norbert R. Schady, 'Aggregate Income Shocks and Infant Mortality in the Developing World', *Policy Research Working Paper*, no. 4346, World Bank, Washington, D.C., 2007; Baldacci, Emanuele, et al., 'Social Spending, Human Capital, and Growth in Developing Countries: Implications for achieving the MDGs', *World Development*, vol. 36, no. 8, 2008, pp. 1317–1341; Barham, Tania, 'Providing a Healthier Start to Life: The impact of conditional cash transfers on neo-natal and infant mortality', Mimeo, Department of Economics and Institute of Behavioral Science, University of Colorado, Boulder, 2006, pp. 1, 25; Ferreira, Francisco, and Norbert R. Schady, 'Aggregate Economic Shocks, Child Schooling and Health', *World Bank Policy Research Working Paper*, no. 4701, Washington, D.C., 2000, p. 26; Fiszbei, Ariel, Paula Inés Giovagnoli and Isidro Adúriz, 'The Argentine Crisis and its Impact on Household Welfare', *CEPAL Review*, no. 79, April 2003, pp. 143–158; Knowles, James, Ernesto Pernia and Mary Racelis, 'Social Consequences of the Financial Crisis in Asia', *Asian Development Bank Economic Staff Paper*, no. 60, Manila, 1999, pp. 43–44; Lustig, Nora,

'Thought for Food: The challenges of coping with soaring food prices', *Center for Global Development Working Paper*, no. 155, Washington, D.C., 2008, p. 33; Macinko, James, et al., 'Going to Scale with Community-Based Primary Care: An analysis of the family health program and infant mortality in Brazil, 1999–2004', *Social Science and Medicine*, no. 65, 2007, pp. 2070–2080; Paxson, Christina, and Norbert R. Shady, 'Child Health and the 1988–92 Economic Crisis in Peru', *World Bank Policy Research Working Paper*, no. 3260, Washington, D.C., March 2004; Galasso, Emanuela, and Martin Ravallion, 'Social Protection in a Crisis: Argentina's *Plan Jefes y Jefas*', *World Bank Policy Research Working Paper*, no. 3165, World Bank, Washington, D.C., November 2003, pp. 1, 3, 23.

Protecting children's rights in humanitarian crises

United Nations Children's Fund, 'Medium Term Strategic Plan 2006–2009, Thematic Humanitarian Report: UNICEF's Humanitarian Assistance in 2008', Office of Emergency Programmes, UNICEF, New York, April 2009, p. 2; Office of the Special Representative of the Secretary-General for Children and Armed Conflict, United Nations Children's Fund, *Machel Study 10-Year Strategic Review: Children and conflict in a changing world*, OSRSG-CAAC and UNICEF, New York, April, 2009, pp.19, 122; William, J. Moss et al., *Child Health in Complex Emergencies, Bulletin of the World Health Organization Policy and Practice*, vol. 84, no. 1, 2006, p. 59; Office of the Special Representative of the Secretary-General for Children and Armed Conflict, United Nations Children's Fund, *Machel Study 10-Year Strategic Review: Children and conflict in a changing world*, OSRSG-CAAC, UNICEF, New York, April, 2009, p. 112; United Nations Children's Fund, *The State of the World's Children 2005: Childhood under threat*, UNICEF, New York, 2004, p. 62.

Climate change and child rights

UNICEF United Kingdom, *Our Climate, Our Children, Our Responsibility: The implications of climate change for the world's children*, UNICEF, London, 2008, pp. 3, 12, 18, 30–31, 33; UNICEF Innocenti Research Centre, *Climate Change and Children: A human security challenge*, Policy Review Paper, UNICEF IRC, in cooperation with UNICEF Programme Division, Florence and New York, November 2008, pp. ix, 2, 4, 12, 13, 22, 41; Derived from United Nations Children's Fund, *The State of the World's Children 2009: Maternal and newborn health*, UNICEF, New York, December 2008, pp. 121, 141; Smith, Dan, and Janani Vivekananda, *A Climate of Conflict: The links between climate change, peace and war*, International Alert, London, November 2007, p. 3; United Nations Children's Fund and Office of the Special Representative of the Secretary-General for Children and Armed Conflict, *Machel Study 10-Year Strategic Review: Children and conflict in a changing world*, UNICEF, New York, April 2009, p. 28; United Nations Development Programme, *Human Development Report 2007/2008: Fighting climate change – Human solidarity in a changing world*, UNDP, 2007, New York, p. 21; Goodman, Donna, 'Water, Sanitation and Hygiene Education ... Children and Adolescents Leading the Way in Tajikistan', United Nations Children's Fund, Water, Environment and Sanitation Section, Programme Division, New York, August 2005, p. 5.

Child rights in Mexico

Economist Intelligence Unit, 'Mexico Country Profile 2008', EIU, London, 2008, p. 15; Concluding Observations of the Committee on the Rights of the Child, Mexico, UN Document CRC/C/15/Add.112 (1999), no. 3, p. 3; Concluding Observations of the Committee on the Rights of the Child, Mexico, UN Document CRC/C/125/Add.7 (December 2004), pp. 6, 66–67; United Nations Children's Fund, *The State of the World's Children 2008: Child survival*, UNICEF, New York, December 2007, p. 38; Behrman, Jere, Piyali Sengupta and Petra Todd, 'Progressing through PROGRESA: An impact assessment of a school subsidy experiment in rural Mexico', *Economic Development and Cultural Change*, vol. 54, no. 1, 2005, pp. 237–275; Oportunidades official website, <www.oportunidades.gob.mx/>, accessed 20 March 2009; Aitken, Stuart, et al., 'Reproducing Life and Labor: Global processes and working children in Tijuana, Mexico', *Childhood*, vol. 13, no. 3, 2006, pp. 365–387; World Bank, Poverty in Mexico – Fact Sheet, <http://go.worldbank.org/MDXERW23U0>, accessed 30 June 2009; UNICEF Mexico Annual Report, 2008, pp. 5–6; Economic and Social Council, 'Indigenous Issues: Human rights and indigenous issues – Report of the Special Rapporteur on the situation of human rights and fundamental freedoms of indigenous people, Rodolfo Stavenhagen, Addendum, Mission to Mexico', United Nations, E/CN.4/2004/80/Add.2, 23 December 2003, p. 17.

Child rights in Mozambique

UNICEF Mozambique, *Mozambique Annual Report 2008*, UNICEF, Maputo, February 2009, p. 7; United Nations Children's Fund, *The State of the World's Children 2009: Maternal and newborn health*, UNICEF, New York, pp. 139, 143; Plano Nacional de Acção para a Criança,

República de Moçambique, Ministério da Mulher e da Acção Social, 2006; Plano de Acção para as Crianças Órfãs e Vulneráveis, República de Moçambique, Ministério da Mulher e da Acção Social, 2006; Impacto Demografico do HIV/SIDA em Mocambique, Ronda de Vigilencia Epidemiologica, 2007'.

Child rights in Serbia

United Nations Children's Fund, *The State of the World's Children 2009: Maternal and newborn health*, UNICEF, New York, 2008, p. 128; United Nations Children's Fund, *UNICEF Serbia Annual Report 2008*, UNICEF, Belgrade, 2008, pp. 6, 9; United Nations Children's Fund, *The State of Children in Serbia 2006: Poor and excluded children*, UNICEF Belgrade, 2007, pp. 17–25; Ahern, Laurie, and Eric Rosenthal, *Torment Not Treatment: Serbia's segregation and abuse of children and adults with disabilities*, Mental Disability Rights International, Washington, D.C., 2007, pp. iii, 5; Kovačević, Vera, 'Child Care System Reform: Serbia Country Assessment', UNICEF Regional Office for CEE/CIS, Geneva, June 2007, pp. iii, 5, 23–25.

Child rights in Sweden

United Nations, 'Human Development Index – Trends', UN, New York, 2009, <http://data.un.org/Document Data.aspx?id=115>, accessed 2 June 2009; UNICEF Innocenti Research Centre, *The Child Care Transition*, Report Card No. 8, UNICEF IRC, Florence, 2008, p. 2; Ministry of Education and Science, Stockholm, Sweden, 'Early Childhood Education and Care Policy in Sweden', Paper presented at the International OECD conference Lifelong Learning as an Affordable Investment, 6–8 December 2000, Ottawa, Canada; Ministry of Health and Social Affairs, 'Strategy to Implement the UN Convention on the Rights of the Child', Fact Sheet No. 6, Ministry of Health and Social Affairs, Sweden, March 2004, p. 2; Committee on the Rights of the Child, 'Consideration of Reports Submitted by States Parties under Article 44 of the Convention: Concluding observations – Sweden', United Nations, 12 June 2009, paragraphs 11–12, 17–18.